THE
GOLDEN
PATHWAY

DR. PHILIP CHAPMAN

BOOKS ACADEMY
LEARNING LIFE FROM EVERY PAGE

Books Academy LLC
112 SW H K Dodgen Loop, Temple, Texas 76504
Hotline: (254) 800-1189

Author: The author, Phil Chapman served as a Chaplain for 29 years. Dr. Chapman graduated from the University of Illinois with Honors, earned a Master's of Criminal Justice from the University of South Carolina graduating Cum Laude and as a Distinguished Honor Graduate, and earned a Doctor's of Ministry from the Chicago Theological Seminary. Educated a scientific rationalist, with some research experience, Phil shares mystical and supernatural experiences.

Ordering Information:
Quantity sales. Special discounts are available on quantity purchases by corporations, associations, and others. For details, contact the publisher at the address above.

Printed in the United States of America.

ISBN-13:   Softcover   979-8-89043-577-4
            eBook   979-8-89043-578-1

MY PRAYER

Lord God Almighty, may Your hand be upon me indeed. Use *The Golden Pathway* to encourage and edify people. May Your hand be upon me so this book causes no pain or harm. Bless my efforts to serve Your will. May this book advance Your kingdom. Amen.

CHARITY

Dr. Chapman will donate 20 percent of the author's portion of profits to 501(C)(3) charities as provided by Section 170 of the United States Federal Tax Code.

CONTENTS

Chapter 1: Stairway to Heaven 1
Chapter 2: The Golden Pathway.....................................5
Chapter 3: Be Still and Know I am God 8
Chapter 4: Angels in the Cold War 12
Chapter 5: Déjà Vu—My First Precognitive Dream 16
Chapter 6: Ghostly Vision at Hohenfels........................18
Chapter 7: Striped Locomotive 22
Chapter 8: Ever Ignore Your Intuition? 24
Chapter 9: Something More—A Trip to the Funeral Parlor........26
Chapter 10: Bluebird?..29
Chapter 11: A Haunted Tiepin? 32
Chapter 12: A Lingering Farewell 35
Chapter 13: Cigarette Smoke Goodbye..........................37
Chapter 14: Unusual Visits 41
Chapter 15: Only a Dove? 43
Chapter 16: My Christmas Angel.................................45
Chapter 17: I Must Go Check on Him Now! 48
Chapter 18: Choose Life! 50
Chapter 19: Look Behind You!....................................53
Chapter 20: Lincoln's Ghost? 56
Chapter 21: Behold, I Make All Things New! 59
Chapter 22: President Lincoln and Senator Dirksen—
           Co-laborers in God's Vineyard....................62
Chapter 23: The Wind Blows Where It Will....................66
Chapter 24: You Reap What You Sow..........................68
Chapter 25: More than They Bargained For...................70
Chapter 26: An Unwanted Visitor 72

Chapter 27: Warning—Dangers of the Occult.............................74
Chapter 28: Dream of Warning? The Capitol Building................76
Chapter 29: An Eagle's Call 79
Chapter 30: A Celestial Dance: The Music of the Spheres............82
Chapter 31: Meditation 85
Chapter 32: Coincidence or the Power of Prayer?........................87

Bibliography...91

CHAPTER 1

Stairway to Heaven

The following story from a ministry in Germany suggests visions may come at unexpected places and times. The US Army provided me a versatile Willys Jeep (WWII style) to conduct my duties. One muddy spring morning, my driver and I purchased brötchen and salami in a small rural town. Low dark rain clouds greeted us as we left the *bakerei* and the *metzgerei* for the countryside. We chose a crushed gravel road that skirted a small chapel nestled in a tree line to visit Delta Company.

Painted white, adorned with the Christian symbolism of clear beehive glass windows, it brightened our dreary day. A local shepherd with a hat cocked to one side wore a woolen cloak pulled tightly about him to protect against the elements. He tended his sheep with gentle words. Occasionally he whistled to his dog which darted in and out the flock, nipping at the sheep's heels. In this way, the flock in his care moved slowly toward new, fresh, tender grass higher on the hillside.

German chapel.

My driver parked the jeep and stayed inside the vehicle, eagerly eating our excellent German fare. I got out and investigated. Peering through the beehive windows, I discovered an oaken stairway leading upward into the grayness. In the dim light I could only see up to the seventh stair. Marveling at its perfect craftsmanship, I wondered, *Where does it lead?* I thought, *There must be a choir loft.* Desiring a closer look, I tried opening the front door. Finding the chapel securely locked, I decided to return the next day.

Stairway to heaven.

We returned to the chapel the next day. Upon my return, I found the perfectly matched oaken doors unlocked. I entered and discovered lacquered pews flanking a carpeted aisle leading to a chancel adorned with colorful floral arrangements. In front of the altar, attired in a white gown and blue cloak, stood a statue of the queen of heaven. A sign at the Virgin's feet read, "Maria Salve."

The townspeople carefully placed two dark picture frames with newspaper clippings which contrasted with the stark white walls. Within the frames, I found the rosters of local German soldiers lost in World War II. These rosters, in old German script, provided each soldier's name and their date of death. One list provided the names of soldiers lost on the eastern front in Rusland. The other provided the names of those lost on the western front in France. The stairway I'd seen the previous day had disappeared!

I stood and reflected on the beautiful chapel built by grieving family members and a perfectly crafted stairway unmade by human hands no longer visible to my eye. The chapel serves as a constant prayer and memorial for those lost on each front during World War II. This chapel remains a place in which the eternal and transitory coincide.

The stairway vision has meaning. As holy ground, where the Word is preached, the chapel is one place in which soldiers may begin their upward climb toward heaven. Soldiers from all epochs and nations who believe in Jesus Christ in a chapel may choose to take their first steps to paradise. Death in combat is not the end. There is something more than the grave. There is eternal life in Christ Jesus.

> And he had a dream. He saw steps going up from the earth to heaven. He saw angels of God going up and down those steps. (Genesis 28:12, NLV)

> And they said, believe on the Lord Jesus Christ, anf thou shalt be saved, and thy family. (Acts 16:31, KJV, Public Domain)

Therefore my beloved bretheren, be ye steadfast, unmovable, always abounding in the work of the Lord, for as much as ye know that your labor is not in vain in the Lord. (I Cor. 15:58, Public Domain).

And the street of the city, was pure gold, as it was transparent glass. (Rev. 21:2, KJV, Public Domain).

CHAPTER 2

The Golden Pathway

The Army billeted me at Fort Jackson while I earned my master's degree at the University of South Carolina. I jogged the beautiful Fort Jackson golf course to stay in shape. One morning I returned from my nine-mile jog and cooled down in my backyard. My clothes drenched in sweat and with a troubled mind, I thought of a close relative suffering from cancer. I looked through the pines skyward and asked the Lord, "If there is eternal life, please give me a sign." My clothes clung to my skin, but on that hot sultry day a cool breeze suddenly sprang up, rustling the treetops. The breeze ended as abruptly as it started. I thought I'd received my answer.

Later that evening I hit the sack and fell into a deep sleep. I awoke as the bedside clock displayed 3:16 a.m. I sat up on the side of the bed and looked out the second-story window to the backyard below. Dressed in black, a hooded figure, with face concealed, stood at the foot of a gleaming golden pathway leading upward into the heavens. The figure beckoned.

The angel of death.

I stood at the foot of a golden pathway. Transfixed, I gazed skyward. The shining bridge led through pine branches narrowing to a gilded portal at the highest reaches of the heavens. A luminescent golden archway led to a glittering silver portal. The portal burned brightly and glistened with the Shekinah of the Lord. I beheld eternity. I saw the entrance to God's throne.

The figure standing at the foot of the golden pathway transported me back to my room. Its countenance concealed, I felt he looked deeply into me. My visitor disappeared behind a large pine tree. The gleaming bridge into the heavens disappeared. A voice commanded, *Go about your work!*

Released from the vision, I regained normal consciousness. I sat on the side of the bed; the lights were on, and the blinds were closed. I wondered how I could have seen out the window with the blinds closed. I got up and started to study. I would graduate from the University of South Carolina's two-year master's of criminal justice program in eleven months. I earned straight As and received a plaque inscribed with the words, "Distinguished Honor Graduate." Later, I finished my work as a prison chaplain after twenty years.

I think of the dark messenger as an angel of death. Death is but the gateway to another world. His servants climb the golden path. Of great worth and of more value than shining gold is a path of service. The path shines brightly for all to see. He showed me a golden pathway to eternal life. We determine our eternal destiny by whom we believe in and how we live our life. Even now, the living may walk toward the foot of Jacob's ladder.

Servants, be about your work. The seeds of the future are present in the present. Narrow is the pathway which leads to life.

The golden pathway: a vision.

And he dreamed, and behold a ladder set up upon the earth, and the top of it reached to heaven, : and behold the angels of God ascending and descending on it. (Gen. 28:12, KJV, Public Domain)

Go through the narrow door, the door is wide and the road is easy that leads to hell. Many people are going through the door. But the road is narrow and the road hard that leads to life that lasts forever and few people are finding it. (Mt. 7:13, NLV)

And God shall wipe away all tears from their eyes; and there shall be no more death, neither sorrow nor crying, neither shall there be anymore pain: for the former things are passed away. And he that sat upon the throne said, Behold I make all things new. (Rev. 21:45, KJV, Public Domain)

CHAPTER 3

Be Still and Know I am God

In the summer of 1985, I proudly served with a mechanized infantry unit in the Federal Republic of Germany (FRG). The infantry trained to shoot, move, and communicate. We protected Europe from a Soviet incursion in the Fulda Gap. I enjoyed the beauty of the German countryside.

Germany's fields and forests seem unsurpassed in their beauty. Our travels brought us into the German heartland. We kept our armored personnel carriers and vehicles off the farmer's fields but frequently camped in forested areas of protection neatly kept by the forest masters who trimmed the tall pines and cleared out the undergrowth. Our units could live comfortably under a canopy of trees hidden from the prying eyes of Russki spies, should the balloon go up. We took our mission to defend Germany seriously.

On one maneuver, I attended the daily briefing and learned a high-pressure front would bring a warm ideal summer evening with cloudless skies with 100% illumination provided by a full moon. I liked this, as it afforded ideal sleeping weather under the stars.

As evening approached, we headed away from town to find an area to camp. Darkness came. Our jeep crept along the fields toward a thicket of tall pines outlined by bright moonlight. Upon arriving at the thicket, we drove deep into the woods under a dense forest canopy. We parked the jeep, and I walked through the pine grove searching for a suitable spot to place a Ranger roll. I strode quietly, only occasionally hearing a snapping of twigs. I smelled the lush fragrance of pines mingling with the musty forest floor. I abruptly stopped standing motionless, transfixed by a clear shaft of silver light.

Silver moonbeam.

A moonbeam split the darkness and formed a silver circlet on the forest floor. The moonbeam's bold-and-sudden appearance spoke of a presence. Looking up, I asked softly, "Is that You, Lord?" After a brief silence, I inquired once again, more insistently, "Is that You, Lord?"

I stepped slowly into the moonbeam and stood in the center of the radiant silver circle. I gazed into the sky and beheld the old familiar countenance of the man on the moon. I had seen the moon thousands of times but never with such clarity. Awed, I mused, "For thirty-five years, I've seen the moon but never really *seen* it!"

The Man In the Moon.

Our unit managed its time effectively and trained with great efficiency to kill our fellow man. Yet suddenly removed from the hectic pace of battalion activity and the exhausting pace of maneuvers, time slowed down, ground to a halt, and then seemed to altogether cease. I stood confronted with God's magnificent creation.

I recalled the words: "Be still and know I am God" (Psalm 46:10).

"When I look up and think about your heavens, the work of your fingers, the moon and the stars, which you have set in their place, what is man that you think of him, the Son of Man that you care for him?" (Ps. 8:3, NLV)

The Creator spoke to me that night. The Creator's love is reflected in His creation. It is God that created us, and we did not create Him. It is He that lights our path.

Ps. 19:1 exclaims; "The heavens are telling the greatness of God and the great open spaces ahow the work of his hands. Day to day they speak, and night to night they show much learning." (NLV)

Ironically, God speaks to us each day in silent words. God's words go to the ends of the earth, boldly proclaiming, "I love you." These words are spoken in a myriad of ways. Though I enjoyed cre-ation for many years, I didn't hear His words reflected in creation. Now I see we enjoy an immense universe. God nurtures and succors man amid the galaxies of stars.

We depend upon a beautiful, incredibly complex yet fragile ecosystem which He sustains. He provides mankind with everything for a life of abundance. Man now seeks to provide for a burgeoning population. We must take care not to destroy ourselves or His creations with weapons of mass destruction, irresponsible use of fossil fuels, chemicals, or other poisons.

The heavens and all of His creation speak with a silent yet deaf-ening voice, whispering, "God loves you!" Mankind should manage the earth with the same deliberate purpose and care the German for-est masters manage their forests. Mankind, created in God's image, may harness but not destroy His created order. Mankind must not take itself too seriously. Ps 8:4 "What is man that you think of him?" (NLV)

Ps 103:15 tells us; "The days of man are like grass. He grows like a flower of the field. When the wind blows over it is gone. It's place will remember him no more." (NLV)

In pride or in folly, the people of the earth must not poison God's earth. Or earth may know us no more. Steward, take a moment and behold the wonder of creation. Take a moment and be changed.

Ps. 46:10 encourages; "Be quiet and know that I am God." (NLV)

CHAPTER 4

Angels in the Cold War

I served as an army chaplain stationed at Böblingen in the Federal Republic of Germany from 1984–1986. Upon my arrival, I quickly surmised that the chapel's upkeep had not been the previous commander's priority. As a battalion and community chaplain, I worked with the command to repair and beautify a dirty and deteriorating chapel. We accomplished numerous improvements and raised over thirty thousand dollars to install specially ordered and designed stained glass windows for the main worship areas.

One bright summer morning shortly after I arrived in Germany, I parked my blue Plymouth Reliant in the parking lot. I entered the weathered oak side door and walked over the dirty orange carpet to my office. I surveyed the room; everything seemed to be exactly as I'd left it the previous day. I looked up through the window, amazed to find a huge, round face with keen eyes peering inside at me. As if no longer part of normal time and space, I entered a strange sort of awareness. I stared at the visage until he moved away from the window.

I moved like a sleepwalker toward the window. Outside, trees our German hosts had carefully planted along the redbrick road used by our track vehicles reached skyward. Sunlight filled the grassy churchyard. Powerful and muscular, he stood dressed in ancient Roman battledress. He wore a coarse homespun tunic which covered his massive chest and thighs, almost down to his knees. Secured over his tunic, he wore a dark leather hauberk and a leather belt from which he hung a Roman short sword known as a Gladius.

An angel from Mons?

He stood some thirty-five feet tall. His head stood level with the treetops. His piercing eyes looked deeply into me. No words were spoken. After a short time, I began to shake my head from side to side and returned to normal time. I wondered what the angel's visitation might mean.

I took the angel's visitation as an auspicious sign. The angel did not appear in full battle gear but engaged me with a kindly countenance. However, it was not until later that I began to see what the visitation might mean. In 1985, the United States stood face-to-face against the Soviet Union in the Cold War. America faced a dangerous and determined opponent. The Soviets, excellently equipped, outnumbered us. Soviet military doctrine posited nuclear war was winnable. The Soviets hoped to gobble up Europe and arrive at the English Channel in less than ten days. The Soviets believed if they invaded an opponent with sufficient armor, and if we employed tactical nukes, they could button up and survive. Ridiculous. American engineer battalions drew up contingency plans for bulldozers to dig mass graves for the tens of thousands of casualties. In the mid-1980s, the world stood on the brink of nuclear annihilation. Thank God we survived. In retrospect, I consider it absurd anyone considered nuclear war as winnable.

In the midst of Cold War Europe, I prepared my sermons. An avid reader of history, I began to understand the angel's appearance when I happened upon the story of the Angels at Mons. In the early days of World War I, superior German firepower and manpower pushed back, retreating French and British troops at Mons. During the days of August 26–28, 1914, the Germans mercilessly pressed their advantage. The allied forces, in a full-scale retreat, began to crumble.

Suddenly, in the midst of the slaughter, allied soldiers reportedly saw huge angels wielding swords and shouting, "Victory!" French soldiers reported seeing St. Michael, while the British forces reported seeing St. George. One soldier reported "a luminous angel with outstretched wings." Strangely, as the allied forces fell apart in disarray, the Germans reported seeing several regiments of allied soldiers resolutely barring their advance. Afterward, psychologists and newsmen provided scientific explanations ranging from battle shock to mass hysteria for the events at Mons. However, those actually present allegedly reported angels.

I humbly suggest I may only understand the angel's appearance at Böblingen Chapel in light of the Angels at Mons. In the early 1980s, America stood the watch in Europe. Although highly trained and ably led, our troops, like those at Mons, stood outnumbered and outgunned. Perhaps we enjoyed the unseen protection of angels among us, which confounded the enemy host.

Psalm 91:9-11 reads; "Because you have made the Lord your safe place, and the Most High the place where you live, nothing shall hurt you. No trouble will come near your tent. For he will tell his angels to care for you and keep you in all his ways." (NLV)

The Enemy that Is Not an Enemy

During the Cold War in Europe, we faced "an enemy who is not an enemy." The Russian people lived oppressed by a totalitarian system which persecuted people of conscience and failed to provide democracy, wealth, or security. If angels protected the free peoples in Cold War Europe, they also served to protect the Russian innocents who would have suffered most cruelly in a conflict with NATO. Perhaps, in a wider sense, unseen angels protect all of humankind from man's inhumanity to man. I hope we never return to a Cold War with the Soviets or China but instead find ways to work together for a peaceful world which cooperatively shares the planet's resources and honors the natural God-given rights of man.

A Geo Political Meaning for 2024 and Beyond

This vision appears to take on additional meaning as free nations face challenges from Russia and China in 2023. Our world remains divided by ideologies and oppressive governments. As Christ taught, "a house divided against itself can't stand." A united world which ensures the natural rights of man for all races, colors, and creeds will prosper. Unfortunately, mankind now has the capability to destroy itself. I hope America is not forced to return to a Cold War with a Russian, Chinese, Iranian, and North Korean Axis.

CHAPTER 5

Déjà Vu—My First Precognitive Dream

My third-grade teacher, Miss McMartin, sat at her desk in front of the room underneath Washington's picture, grading papers. Her students worked diligently at their desks. A strict disciplinarian, Miss Mac, as we called her, didn't allow talking in class. You could have heard a pin drop in Mac's class when the tip of my pencil broke with a loud snap!

I raised my hand and asked to sharpen my pencils. Three pencils in hand, I walked to the sharpener positioned alongside the window ledge. I looked out the window and felt strange. I thought, *I have been here before.* I wondered how I already had looked at the scene outside. Another boy holding two pencils in his hand walked to the sharpener. He smiled and gestured to me. The scene continued to unfold exactly as I dreamed previously. I inserted my pencil and ground it to a sharp point. Removing it from the sharpener, I found the tip flawed. I decided this was an experience of note. Afterward, I shared what had happened with Miss Mac. She smiled and listened intently to my story and told me to return to my seat.

I forgot about my experience until later in the week. Miss Mac proudly announced our entire class would see a film in the auditorium. All the kids in the class knew this was a big deal. We only went to the auditorium for important events! Once inside, I sat in a large cushioned seat and felt dwarfed by the spacious auditorium. I looked up at the huge white screen on the stage. Miss Mac walked to the podium in her plain cotton dress and proudly announced we'd all see a movie about dreams.

The lights went out. We viewed an entertaining movie featuring child actors depicting young people's dreams with hilarious nonsensical plots. We all laughed. The movie never mentioned Sigmund Freud, C.G. Jung, or the word *precognition* (which probably would have confused all of us). Ironically, after having viewed the movie, the only explanation I had about the meaning of dreams was that there was no meaning! I thought dreams appeared to be utter nonsense.

The film ended. I stood up to leave the auditorium when Mr. Duncan, our beloved school principal, appeared. He looked down at me kindly and asked if I enjoyed the movie. I replied yes. After all, given what I had reported to Miss Mac, I knew the only reason we saw the movie was because of me! The educational systems' systematic eradication of my sixth sense had begun.

Many years would pass until I sought to develop my spirituality through meditation techniques. My natural paranormal ability developed through the eons and passed on through my mother's genes, reemerged later. Some do not have the ability. Others have it and deny it. Others experience the paranormal and repress it. Others choose to experience it within safe limits. Some appear devoured by it. I think our beloved Miss Mac and Mr. Duncan, who've gone on to their reward, would now agree that déjà vu exists.

Ever experience a déjà vu? You're not alone.

CHAPTER **6**

Ghostly Vision at Hohenfels

I served as battalion chaplain for the mechanized infantry stationed at Panzer Kaserne, Böblingen, Federal Republic of Germany (FRG) in the mid-1980s. Our unit frequently went on maneuvers. During my first trip to Hohenfels' training area, I lost the use of my jeep because a company commander's jeep's radiator punctured in a freak accident. The company commander got my jeep.

Our battalion commander suggested I establish a working relationship with our Command Sergeant Major (CSM) better and that we share the CSM's jeep until mine was repaired. A commander's suggestion is the same as an order. I linked up with the CSM at the appointed hour, and we rode and visited units together.

CSM taught the NCOS and soldiers how to prepare positions by digging in, camouflaging, establishing communications, ensuring interlocking fire, and creating kill zones. The CSM enjoyed cigars and spoke about his experience as both a German and later as an American soldier. Occasionally, I helped soldiers dig double foxholes designed with sturdy overhead protection and grenade sumps. This work helped me gain respect of the enlisted men. Thus, I handed out New Testaments to the soldiers, listened to their problems, and got to know the men.

During our travel to the training center, I heard about Castle Hohenfels. Always interested in history, I asked sergeant major if we

18

could visit it, but other responsibilities kept us from visiting the castle. I kept bugging him until finally he said, "Okay, Chaplain, we'll go see the ruins." Delighted and very pleased that he would honor my request, we set off to our destination. The sun shone through the tall German pines. Beautiful pastoral scenes unfolded around each bend in the road. We chatted, and the CSM shared personal stories from his long military career. He knew all the roads at Hohenfels. Finally, we drove up a knoll, and upon arriving at the hilltop, CSM stopped the jeep and said, "Well, there it is, sir!" We got out of the jeep.

I saw a modest stone castle. Its design may have been a forerunner to larger castles. There were towers, tall walls with ramparts, and a huge oaken door which served as an entrance to the fortress. Later I would see a castle much like it when I visited Thun in Switzerland. Outside of the castle stood perhaps fifteen figures dressed in black waving black or red flags attached to the ends of five- or six-foot long poles. I stood watching the spectacle and, turning to CSM, I said, "Look, Sergeant Major, there is some sort of a community event going on. I wonder if the people out front are doing a reenactment. Perhaps they are members of the Society of Creative Anachronism. Do you have that here in Germany? What a great castle!"

I sensed one of the members, perhaps the leader, looking straight at me, beckoning me to come and talk. So I said, "Let's go down and meet them, Sergeant Major."

He replied, "No, sir, we can't. We don't have time. I have a meeting with the battalion commander. Besides, the castle is off limits as per the order of the German government!"

I replied, "Oh, come on, Sergeant Major, they're at the castle. Aren't we supposed to form good relationships with the host nation?"

The sergeant major said, "No!" I knew I'd been trumped. He provided good reasons and wasn't going to budge. We returned to battalion headquarters.

The first day upon receiving my jeep back, I charted a course for the castle using the route the CSM taught me. Driving to the top of a small hill, I returned to the exact spot from which we'd originally viewed the castle. I looked only to find there was no castle! The castle had vanished. I did not need to review the coordinates. The landmarks and surroundings were exactly the same. However, the difference I noted seemed rather significant. *No castle!* Astonished, I wondered what this might mean.

Later in the day, I returned to battalion headquarters. I cornered the sergeant major and asked incredulously, "I returned to the castle today, and it was gone. Where did it go?"

He replied, "Sir, the castle was destroyed long ago. There is nothing left but ruins. Only the people with the second sight can see it." Afraid if others knew what I had seen they would think I was using drugs or crazy, I stood dumbfounded. I'd never heard the words "second sight." I did not understand.

Vision of Hohenfels Castle.

Meaning of Ghostly Vision at Hohenfels

Later, I considered why ghosts in black waving red flags appeared to me in front of the castle. I humbly suggest the Lord allows those souls to linger and function as a warning to others. I sense their basic message is, "Do not place your trust in fortresses, modern weapons of mass destruction, or a preoccupation with mate-rial wealth and authority. These things are but for a time. God is the Alpha and Omega. God is from everlasting to everlasting." The following Scriptures encourage us to trust in God.

Psalm 71:1 affirms; "O Lord in thee I put my trust." (KJV, Public Domain)

Psalm 46:1 explains; "God is our refuge a strength, a very present help in trouble." (KJV, Public Domain)

Psalm 31: 2-3 states: "Bow down your ear to me, deliver me speedily, be thou my strong rock, for a house of defense to save me. For thou art my rock and my fortress; therefore, for thy name's sake lead me, and guide me." (KJV, Public Domain)

As each day passes, the world becomes increasingly more hostile. America faces a multiplicity of threats. Many believe in the old Roman adage, "If you desire peace, prepare for war." However, weapons grow old, or may malfunction, and are only as good as the warriors who wield them. Weapons can take but not give life. The Hohenfels Fortress lay in ruins and serves as a sad testimony to those who placed their trust in castles and weapons rather than God.

Psalm 18:2 "The Lord is my rock and fortress."
(KJV, Public Domain)

World leaders and radical violent ideologies must seek a better way. Matthew 5:4 extols, "Blessed are the peacemakers, for they shall be called the children of God." Men and women of good will must seek to divide the earth's resources in a just way which recognizes the rights of man. In this way will we know peace, security, and victory. Those who seek justice and peace will be on the Lord God Almighty's side in a conflict.

CHAPTER 7

Striped Locomotive

I completed chaplains basic training at Fort Monmouth, New Jersey, and the army assigned me to the 2/52 Air Defense Artillery at Fort Bliss, Texas. Upon my arrival at Fort Bliss, the medical system provided excellent dental care. Dentists removed my wisdom teeth (which I will never forget!) and decided to provide me with new upper teeth. The expensive and sophisticated procedure took awhile to complete. Therefore, I made several trips to the dentists' offices situated across post.

I made my appointments on time. On one such day, blue skies, a blazing hot sun, and El Paso's intense dry heat greeted me when I left my office and drove to the good doctor's chair. I hopped into my tin-like Plymouth Reliant (my first new car), turned on the AC, and headed across post.

Nearing the dentist's office, I reached a familiar railroad intersection I'd crossed numerous times. I'd never seen a train on those tracks. Although I anticipated the bumpy tracks, I slowed down only a little, preparing to cross when I heard a commanding voice say, "Stop!" I hit the brake and stopped short of the tracks. I found a striped locomotive approaching from my left. The engineer had not blown the horn. Had I continued, my tiny "Reliant K" might have lost an argument with a diesel locomotive! I could have been killed in a freak accident. Afterwards, I might have been found oozing out the car doors. I'm fortunate I didn't wind up resembling canned spam.

Did an angel of protection warn me? I believe the Lord saved me.

> The angel of the Lord stays close to those who fear Him and He takes them out of trouble. (Psalm 34:7, NLV)

I heard a small voice of warning or a diesel locomotive might have crushed me to death. Was it an angel of protection's voice?
Credit: Brianmcfa. Public Domain File: Union Pacific 6922: jpg

CHAPTER 8

Ever Ignore Your Intuition?

Have you, like me, ever ignored your intuition and paid for it? Long ago, while stopped in city traffic, I noticed a bumper sticker which read, "I stop for animals." See if my story speaks to you.

After making a donation at the hospital thrift store, I sped home outside Greenville, Illinois, along a virtually empty US 40. Traveling in the right lane, I noticed a small box turtle scrambling quickly in the late morning sun across the hot pavement. Despite nonexistent traffic, my intuition told me the turtle was in danger. I feared for the turtle. However, comfortably seated in my Rogue, I rationalized I sped too quickly to stop and safely remove the helpless creature from the road. I passed by it.

My conscience screamed, *The turtle needs help.* After a huge white SUV coming the other way whizzed past me, I turned around and hurried back to save my innocent friend. The SUV, now ahead of me (the only vehicle that had shared US 40 that morning), dwindled rapidly in the distance. I stopped then gently picked up the broken shell and bleeding body of my lifeless friend. I raged at the driver of the white SUV but understood the lifeless body I sadly was my fault. I could have acted and didn't and felt ashamed.

I grew angry at the driver who could have easily avoided the turtle but then understood I failed to listen to my intuition and callously neglected a living being. I really couldn't blame that person's callous disregard for the murdered turtle, but I could take responsibility for failing to stop! With a new awareness of how to use my gift, I joined the Humane Society and visit dogs and cats at a no-kill kill facility to bring love and treats. Many innocent, loving animals need adoption.

The love of the Creator is reflected in His creation. God created us in His image as stewards to protect the world and its creatures. If we reflect a genuine love for the animal kingdom in our treatment of pets, beasts, and the myriad of species across the globe, we become loving cocreators with God. I remain focused on saving and enhancing life. People will make a difference if they care for the smaller creatures around them. Amid the current world extinction event driven by man, animals have a right to live. I learned from my mistake.

> A man who is right with God cares for the animal, but the sinful man is hard and has no pity. (Proverbs 12:10, NLV)

> I will not pass through this life but once. If therefore, there be any kindness I can show, or any good thing that I can do to any fellow-being, let me do it now, and not defer or neglect it, as I will not pass this way again. (Stephen Grellet)

CHAPTER

9

Something More—A Trip to the Funeral Parlor

My mother's death certificate states she died on January 3, 2006. Upon news of her death, I flew into Seattle, rented a car, and battled I-5 corridor traffic northwards to Solie's Funeral Home in Everett, Washington, to make funeral arrangements.

I'd never been to Solie's Funeral Home and hadn't been to Seattle in forty-five years. My mother's side of the family traditionally used Solie's Funeral Home for funerals. The funeral director, a cordial and a helpful man, greeted me upon my arrival.

While waiting for my brother, the director provided me a brief tour of the funeral home. Perhaps hoping to use the opportunity to make yet another satisfied Webb family customer, he whisked me into the showroom, featuring caskets and funeral vaults. The caskets and arrangements offered by Solie's Funeral Home varied in price.

As I surveyed the caskets, I experienced what Freudians coined a déjà vu experience. I knew I'd been in Solie's before and had this very conversation. The room, his words, his face, and the cutaways of the caskets showing casket construction appeared exactly as I'd witnessed in a dream.

Dumbfounded, I turned to him and said, "I don't know what this might mean, but I've been here before. I've seen these caskets and walked through this room with you before. I think it means there is something more after this life. I don't know what is next, but there is something more!" The Solie's representative also believed in an afterlife. Nevertheless, I respectfully declined the director's suggestion that I prearrange my future funeral arrangements at a set price with Solie's.

Days later, I enjoyed the privilege of delivering my mother's eulogy. I wrestled with what to say for many hours. I honored her memory by highlighting her loving care as a mother and her service to her country in World War II. Mom served tirelessly for American veteran's causes later in life. Interestingly, as I looked out upon the congregation. I again caught quick glimpses of a scene I'd previously witnessed. As I had once toured the casket display room, I'd also looked out on the crowd before. I don't pretend to completely understand the déjà vu experience. However, I provide an explanation of déjà vu dreams.

While sleeping, I saw a glimpse of the future. Some dreams appear to be a type of time travel. My sleep seemingly become an altered state of consciousness that catapulted me into significant future events. As I didn't reject nor fear the experience, it proved instructive. Death, a natural part of life, is but a transition. My mother's transition from this life to the next is normal. However, there is more to come than placement in a casket or the scattering of ashes. Unless you led an evil life, death is not to be feared.

Some déjà vu dreams may serve us much like a sign along a road. My dream indicated I traveled the right road. I accomplished part of my destiny when I honored my mother by delivering her eulogy in Everett. Like her, my days, and the very hairs on my head, are numbered. I will take the final trip from this world. The clock is ticking, and my name is on the ticket of departure to something more. I don't see it all clearly now, nor do I know the date and time of my departure; but the train will arrive, and I will make the final journey. I'm sure it'll be an eye opener!

For now we see through a glass darkly, but then face to face, now I know in part, but then shall I know even as also I have known. (I Cor. 23:12, KJV, Public Domain)

Honor your father and mother, as the Lord your God has told you. (Deut 5:16, NLV)

CHAPTER **10**

Bluebird?

The death certificate states my mother, Audrey Anita Webb, died on January 3, 2006. I received the news of her passing somberly. We'd just spoken three days prior on New Year's Eve. On that occasion, she just didn't seem to want the conversation to end. We chatted for a long time. Only later did my brother inform me that she called him earlier in the year to visit with her in Everett to discuss funeral arrangements. He visited, but the conversation concerning funeral arrangements never materialized. At eighty-six, Audrey knew her final journey approached.

The day following news of her death, I got up late. I dressed, went to the kitchen, and started the coffee. Mom loved coffee. The pot gurgled, and the aroma of delicious hazelnut coffee wafted throughout the kitchen. They found her body slumped over on the couch with her hands down by her feet as if she had started to tie her shoes. I remembered she taught me to tie my shoes over fifty years ago.

I filled my red, white, and blue Spinners coffee cup adorned with the American flag and the words "God Bless America" emblazoned on its side. Very patriotic. Mom served in the WACS during WWII and, later in life, worked for veteran's causes into her seventies. Scratching my head, I ambled over to the window and looked out on a blustery January day. The sun shone brightly. Our Colorado

Blue Spruce's branches waved a *good morning* to me in gusting winds. A flock of English sparrows and a lone, brilliantly plumed red cardinal feverishly feasted at the hanging feeder.

Duly noting the presence of my feathered guests, I settled back in a chair at the kitchen table. My perch provided a lovely panoramic view of the yard. The lawn's gently sloping hill led to the glistening lake below. The lake's sparkling waves glittered in the sun's bright morning light. The waves rolled southward toward a rock dam where a gaggle of about fifty Canadian geese enjoyed my neighbor's ration of corn. Gazing outside, I recognized that I just inherited the highly coveted title of oldest generation. Life sometimes moves inexorably to a predetermined end, from which when we, ravaged by old age and time, mercifully find there is no escape. May my generation be the next to go. But not right away!

My mother, though slowed by age, maintained a positive attitude toward life. With a heart as big as the great outdoors, she lived a happy-go-lucky life. Mom loved parties, bright clothes, and the latest news. As a conversationalist, Audrey would talk your ears off. Proud and independent, Mom got up early every morning and worked for a veterans' organization well into her late seventies. I mused upon Mom's contributions to our world when a small-feathered creature joined my reverie. A Bluebird flew onto the deck railing then peered into the kitchen directly at me.

Bluebird.

In over six years, I never saw a Bluebird in our yard. I won-dered if powerful winter winds blew my guest off course from a blue-bird's normal range. Surprised and pleased at the bird's appearance, I returned its gaze. My tiny visitor hopped from the railing to a glass table to gain a better view of me. The Bluebird gained my undivided attention. Our eyes locked. My visitor said goodbye. It cocked its head to the side, tapped its beak on the tabletop three times, then gave one last glance and flitted to the nearest balsam.

The Bluebird reminded me of my mother. I stood up, moved to the window, and sighed. "Goodbye, my happy-go-lucky guest." My Bluebird flew southward, out of sight. Perhaps it flew through bright blue skies, beyond the sunset, to an eternal dawn where there is no aging, tears, or death.

> Honor your father and mother, as the Lord your God has told you. (Deut 5:16, NLV)

> As for man his days are like grass; he flourishes like a flower of the field; for the wind passes over it, and it is gone, and its place knows it no more. (Ps. 103:15-16, KJV, Public Domain)

> Let not your heart be troubled; ye believe in God, believe also in me. In my Father's house are many mansions: if it were not so, I would have told you. I go to prepare a place for you. (John 14:1-2 KJV, Public Domain)

> And the street of the city was pure gold, as if it was transparent glass. (Rev. 21:21, KJV, Public Domain)

CHAPTER 11

A Haunted Tiepin?

My grandfather worked the Alaskan railroad as a blacksmith during the summers of the gold rush. A first-generation Norwegian American born in Wausau, Wisconsin, he found the cold climate and higher wages agreeable. Grandpa never struck it rich. According to my mother, he'd leave Swans Trail, Washington, and head north in the spring, and then return in the late summer or fall with the money he'd saved in Alaska.

Grandpa died and didn't leave a lot of money to his heirs. However, in the early 1990s, my mother sent me an old, bent, golden tiepin with a diamond chip mounted on the top. Long past its day, I knew I wouldn't use it, but I placed it respectfully in my jewelry box, along with other sentimental items.

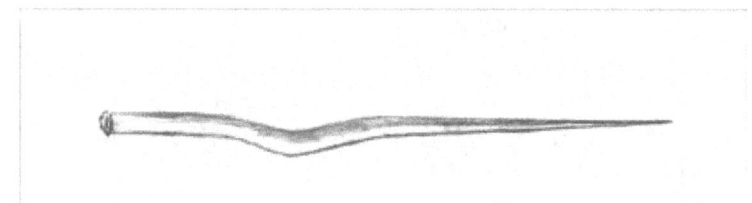

Haunted tiepin.

In the evening, I prepared for bed and fell asleep. Awakened abruptly, I found the room very cold and the covers in a heap at my feet. I sensed a ghostly presence in the room. My covers, moved by an unseen force, seemed cold to the touch. Something or someone invaded my space. Snatching the covers and pulling them up to the head of the bed, I commanded sternly, "Go! You do not belong here. Go back to where you came from and don't come back!" I turned on the lights, readjusted the covers, and turned up the furnace. I thought, *A ghost just visited me.* Undaunted and needing to go to work in the morning, I fell back to sleep.

The next day, I called my mother, Audrey, and described my experience. She replied matter-of-factly, "Philip, I know your experience is true. The scariest night Mac and I ever spent was in our place in Shangri-La, Washington, in our house on the river. Mac and I awoke in the dead of night, freezing cold. The covers were at the foot of the bed. We didn't know what it was. Scared, we turned on every light in the house. We stayed up, eyes wide open until dawn. When I called Pa the next day, he said, 'Audrey that was your mother!'"

Audrey continued saying, "After Ma died, your grandfather experienced something similar. Pa woke up in a cold room with his covers pulled down to the foot of the bed. Sensing someone in the room, he told her a thing or two! Pa told me he loudly barked an order: 'You don't belong here. Go to where you belong and don't come back!' Grandpa knew it was your grandmother, Marguerite. Paw said, 'She left and never came back.'"

Like my grandfather, I'd ordered Grandmother's spirit from the house using almost the exact words he had used many years before. To my knowledge, Grandmother never appeared again. Why Marguerite made her presence known to the four of us in so dramatic a fashion is unknown to me. Perhaps the reason for her visitation is known only to her and unto God. I hope she finds rest.

Marguerite's appearance remains a strange source of encouragement. She served to remind me there is something more after this life. I believe the place we spend eternity in is a result of the choices we make in this life. In addition, her appearance served to remind me of the potentially disastrous consequences of the supernatural in our lives. While experiencing my gift, I stay within the guidelines God commands in Scripture. I stand fast in the Lord.

> Romans 8:28 "And we know that all things work together for the good to them that love God, to them that who are called according to His purpose." (KJV, Public Domain)

CHAPTER 12

A Lingering Farewell

My grandparents, John and Eva, took their wedding vows on August 17, 1917. They celebrated a strong marriage for over sixty years. Healthily, both lived into their eighties. Like many elderly people, they encountered health problems toward the end of their lives. Suffering with ill health, they remained alive to support one another.

After their passing, my father related a story of my grandfather's love for Eva. At my grandmother's funeral, before the undertaker closed the coffin, my grandfather leaned over grandmother's face and kissed her repeatedly. Soon afterward John would also make the journey.

Very close in life, Grandpa and Grandma also remained very close in death. In the aftermath of their passing, I traveled to Wisconsin to visit my father and stepmother. My father inherited my grandparents' summer cottage on a beautiful spring fed lake. Built in the 1920s, my grandparents dubbed it Hillcrest. Hillcrest stood on a bluff overlooking the lake. Upon arrival, I helped clean up, paint, and do some other odd jobs to spruce up the old cottage. At that time, my father gave me some family heirlooms to include a secretary desk, a gateleg table, and a photograph of Abraham Lincoln taken during the 1860 presidential election.

I worked for several days. The evening prior to departure, I bade my farewells and packed the car with my heirlooms. I got up at dawn, dressed, and fortified by a cup of coffee, walked out of the house into the cool morning air. I took one last look toward our beloved lake. A deep gray fog filled the northern woods. The quiet lake concealed below, I saw only the dark silhouettes of the trees in the fog. I started my car and began my descent slowly down a crushed red granite driveway surface. Tall oaks, white birches, and balsams stood like silent sentinels along the driveway. I started the long drive early because I wanted to have plenty of time to unpack and then wash the car before dark.

To my astonishment, suddenly the two familiar faces of Grandpa John and Grandma Eva appeared suspended over the hood. As if posing in a photo booth at a carnival, the two visages floated at windshield level. Grandma, closer and to the left, smiled. Grandpa's stern visage appeared higher to the right and slightly behind Grandma's. Puzzled, I drove slowly down the driveway onto Big Portage Lake access road.

Now transfixed by the ghostly countenances which kept pace ahead of the car, I wondered what their appearances meant. The fog provided a bland backdrop for their faces that neither moved nor changed. I encountered no early morning traffic. My grandparents' visages escorted me down the access road, onto a county road, to the outskirts of town. Upon reaching the outskirts of Land O' Lakes, they vanished abruptly as they had appeared. I never saw their faces again. I shall always remember their lingering farewell. After this mortal life, there is something more.

CHAPTER **13**

Cigarette Smoke Goodbye

The phone rang loudly in the middle of the night. Startled from deep sleep, I turned groggily and picked it up. My father once told me if the phone rings in the middle of the night, it's never good news. It wasn't. My brother told me, "Dad is dead."

I wasn't surprised. My dad, a successful government administrator, loved the good life, which he equated to smoking, drinking, and partying. In his seventies and eighties, the bill came due, and he paid for it with his physical and mental health. Dad once told me, "If I can't do all the things I like [translation: bad habits], life will be no fun. I'd rather die." Now he had. Dead on an emergency room gurney, he'd said goodbye to his wife, waited for her to leave, and then, "checked out of this world." I took the news with a quiet equanimity and stoic dignity. I didn't cry, and I looked at the ceiling, feeling relieved. I would no longer have to serve as his inflatable Bozo the Clown bop bag.

Although I would visit him and my stepmom every year, we weren't emotionally close. My father, an alcoholic and a narcissist, always found fault with me. As a child in an alcoholic family—while others got to play the role of hero or clown—I was relegated the coveted role of scapegoat. After the brief phone call ended, I simply stared at the ceiling thinking. My memories weren't happy. As the son of a me-first-you-last narcissist, Dad wanted to live through his children. He wanted me to be a lawyer. I chose ministry. He never forgave me.

When during the summers I'd visit him in Wisconsin, he'd remind me of his displeasure. One evening, after supper we stood out back talking. After supper, we stood out back, talking. He drank a number of good ones. He loved a good stiff drink (frequently, doubles). His mood grew ugly. A Dr.-Jekyll-and-Mr.-Hyde sort of drunk, he waited for the right moment when his altered personality sprang its trap. He turned to me and sneered. "You're a flop. What a disappointment you are."

I replied calmly, "Father, I've always tried to show you respect. You've never been happy with my decisions. You want to live my life for me. You've been very successful in the world and have become wealthy. But as you berate me, perhaps you should consider you might not even be standing here talking if it weren't for me. You probably don't remember, but I saved your life twice. Once, late one night when you were so drunk in Northbrook, after you criticized me and went to bed, something told me to follow you upstairs. I went up the stairs not more than an inch behind you when you stumbled. I held you up under the armpits, protecting you. I'll bet you don't remember I prevented you from tumbling backward down the stairs and killing yourself, because you never said thanks. You could have broken your neck.

"Another time, you were sick and in the hospital. Your lungs were filled with water. You wouldn't listen to anyone and allow your lungs to be pumped out. You could have drowned! I'm sure no one wanted to tell you afterward because then I'd get some credit. Mom called, asking for help. I arranged for her to come pick me up from the seminary. When I arrived at the room, you were on your back in a hospital gown. You sneered disdainfully at me and said, 'Oh, so they sent you.' Then you got out of the bed and, like a trained dancing bear, twirled and did a little two-step with your ass showing. The nurses came and put you back in the bed. I know you don't remember."

He interjected, almost humanly, "No, I only remember being drugged and being in great pain."

I continued, "You were out of your mind. I looked you straight in the eye and said, 'Dad. Look at me. You must listen now. If you don't let them put that tube down your throat, you will die! Look at me. You are killing yourself. Let them put the tube in your throat, or you will die from drowning! Do you understand? Now do you want to live or do you want to die?'

"Coming to your senses, you said, 'I want to live.' I called to the nurses who then arranged for staff to pump the water from your lungs. You don't remember, and you never said thanks. You could be dead. You owe me your life twice. You never knew, and you never said thanks. You survived and had everything in this life, but now you pay a price. Your health is gone. You've got the house of your dreams, but you don't enjoy it. If, by your own choice, you've become an unhappy bird in a gilded cage, please don't take it out on me."

He hoisted his drink. With piercing eyes and a twisted smile, he retorted sardonically, "You've chosen your world, and I've chosen mine. Now let's go in the house and have some fun with everyone else."

My father turned to leave toward the house. I guess he thought I'd driven six hundred miles to visit and be insulted. Incredulous, I laughed. Offended and always wanting to have the last word and inflict as much damage to his child as possible, he turned and took a mockingly haughty tone. "You won't be laughing later when you read the will." That night, at his worst, he verbally sucker punched me and ran away. He'd gone too far.

When I received news of his death, this is the man I remembered. I slowly fell back to sleep. Sometime later, I awoke to the strong smell of cigarette smoke. After a bit, the filthy smell disappeared. My wife never smoked, and I'd quit many years before. My dad used to smoke two packs of Chesterfields and, later, two packs of Kent cigarettes a day. This unmistakable olfactory visitation was dad's way of saying goodbye. Miserable people like company, but not just any company. Miserable people like miserable company.

Later, I would provide my father's eulogy. Have you experienced similar family relationships? I hope the following scriptures provide insight:

> Wine makes people act in foolish ways. Strong drink starts fights. Whoever is fooled by it is not wise. (Proverbs 20:1, NLV)

> Be sober, be vigilant, because your adversary the devil, as a roaring lion walketh about, seeking who he may devour. (I Pet 5:8, KJV, Public Domain)

> Judge not lest ye be judges. Condemn not and ye will be not condemned. Forgive, and ye shall be forgiven. (Luke 6:57, KJV, Public Domain)

> Honor your father and mother. (Exodus 20:12, KJV, Public Domain)

CHAPTER 14

Unusual Visits

My parents divorced in 1960. Every weekend seemed like "the Friday night fights." They hurt each other deeply, and I never saw them together again until over sixty years later.

Having packed my bike and accessories the night before, I woke up early and drove to my bicycling route. I enjoyed twenty miles of beautiful scenery and finished just as it began to get really hot. Returning home, I prepared a light bite to eat and took a hot shower. Tired from the ride and with a number of personal issues plaguing me, I trundled into the bedroom, plopped onto the bed, and turned on the ceiling fan. I fell into a deep slumber.

I awoke suddenly and pulled the sheet covering my face to the side. To my surprise, I gazed at my parents' translucent visages suspended just below the ceiling. With my mother's face to the left of Dad's, their eyes caught mine, and they smiled. My dad departed this world over twenty years ago, while my mother followed some five years later.

Each appeared in the vigor of their thirties. Their faces showed no sign of aging or death. I looked away, and they were gone. I thought their brief visit was encouraging. They cared enough to overcome differences to see me together. They still loved me.

Later that summer, I visited my father's grave. During previous visits to the cemetery, I'd spoken to him, spewing forth contempt and anger. Given his visit with Mom, on that day, my shadow covered his stone. I whispered, "You loved me. I forgive you for the hurt and harm you caused." I walked thoughtfully to my mini SUV and lingered a moment, then drove away. I returned later in the week to clean up his uncared-for grave. I haven't returned since.

> Honor your father and mother. (Exodus:20:12, KJV, Public Domain)

> Then Peter came to Jesus and asked; "Lord, how many times should I forgive my brother or sister who sins against me? Up to seven times?" Jesus answered, "I tell you, not seven times but seventy times seven times." (Mt. 18:21-22, KJV, Public Domain)

CHAPTER 15

Only a Dove?

I left my parent's cottage "Up North" as the dawn's early light crept slowly into the eastern sky. Some two hours later, I hurtled down US 51/I-39 headed south. The interstate revealed magnificent views of lush green forests, the meandering Wisconsin River, and the Rib Mountain with its forested ski trails overlooking Wausau. I chose Wausau's McDonald's to pick up two egg McMuffins and hot coffee. I stretched my legs, started my car, and entered a tangled web of entrance and exit ramps seeking I-39.

Perhaps a bit lackadaisical due to light traffic, I hurried along heedless of any possible peril. I failed to recognize the danger the labyrinth of tangled roads posed. Nevertheless, I found my way back to the I-39 entry ramp and stopped. I prepared to move onto the ramp when I heard a voice command, *Stop!* I jammed on the brakes. I looked right and saw a huge tractor trailer truck doing seventy to forty-five mph zone!

When he noticed me, I saw that good ole boy trucker's eyes open wide! Thus, jolted to my senses, I tensed my body and jammed on the brake. The truck roared by in front of my vehicle. My head and shoulders slumped as I let out a deep breath. Looking to my left, I saw a mourning dove perched on the steel retaining rail but two feet from my car. I wondered, *Do angels appear in the form of birds? Who warned me?*

Angel?

Was this dove an angel? I do not know. At the very least, I see the dove as a symbol of God's Holy Spirit and love. Mark 1:10 reads, "Coming up out of the water, he saw the heavens opened, and the Spirit like a dove descending upon him." I could have easily suffered a tragic accident. Throughout the Bible, doves appear as a symbol of God's grace. I found the dove's appearance auspicious. After many years, I still see the dove as a sign of God's providential care. A loving God preserved my life. Many years later, although I display numerous shortcomings, I sense He has a plan for me.

Parapsychologists might call this experience of a disembodied voice or an audio vision. I call it God's providential care. On at least three distinct occasions, I believe God's agents warned me of an approaching disaster while I drove my car, but I don't understand why. A choir, I know, sings the song, "He's an on Time God." When I needed protection, He came through on time! I did not need to ask. Nevertheless, Scripture calls on us to ask for God's protection.

> Seek ye the Lord and His stregth continually. (I Chron. 16:11, KJV, Public Domain)

> Preserve me O God, for in thee do I put my trust. (Psalm 16:1, KJV, Public Domain)

CHAPTER **16**

My Christmas Angel

In the nineties, our young family really celebrated Christmas! We made no apologies for this. We wasted no time after Thanksgiving holidays in putting up our tree and greenery throughout the house. Previously, while we were still fortunate to have my wife's parents still alive, their children all gathered at a predetermined place. I must confess, there may have been times we went overboard with the materialistic side of the holidays, but by and large, we sought to celebrate the birth of our Lord Jesus Christ.

One Christmas, when I worked as a chaplain at a major penitentiary, true to family tradition, my wife took the children to my brother-in-law's home in Ohio. I did not like this travel arrangement. Selfishly, I thought our nuclear family should celebrate together at our home in Indiana.

On Christmas Eve, following my ministry at the prison, I returned to an empty house. Alone and a bit melancholic, I sought Christmas cheer by listening to my favorite Christmas carols performed by the Mormon Tabernacle Choir, Nat King Cole, and Bing Crosby. I read in the living room, periodically pausing to admire our dazzling Christmas tree placed carefully by the living room window. I loved the twinkling lights and ornaments of various sizes, colors, and shapes which adorned the tree.

We collected a myriad of ornaments throughout the years. Some of our ornaments came from Kathy Wolfhart's Christmas store in the ancient walled city of Rothenberg on the Tauber in Germany. Others, we created or made ourselves. One ornament I love is made in the shape of an oval. In the middle is a white candle, surrounded by holly at the base, whose flickering red flame provides a serene yellow light. I believe this ornament symbolizes the light and wisdom which came into the world at Christmas. Toward the end of the evening, I looked up at this same ornament, and instead of seeing the candle in the middle of the oval, I encountered the visage of an angel who did not speak. I gazed at his fair countenance. I fell asleep.

"And there were in the same country shepherds abiding in the fields, keeping watch over their flocks b night. And, lo an angel of the Lord came upon them, and the glory of the Lord shone round about them, : and they were sore afraid. And the angel said to them, Fear not, for Behold I bring you tidings of great joy, which shall be to all people. For unto you you is born this day in the City of David a savior, which is Christ the Lord. And this will be sign to you. You shall find a babe wrapped in swaddling clths an lying in a manger." (Luke 2:8-12, KJV, Public Domain)

Are you feeling deserted by those closest to you? Do your responsibilities stress you out? Do you sometimes think, *Stop the world. I want to get off?* Facing difficult odds? Getting worn out?

Isaiah 9:2 tells us; "The people walking in darkness have seen a great light, on those living in a land of deep darkness a light has dawned." (KJV, Public Domain)

Jesus tells us in John 16:35, "In the world you will have much trouble. But take hope! I have power over the world." (NLV)

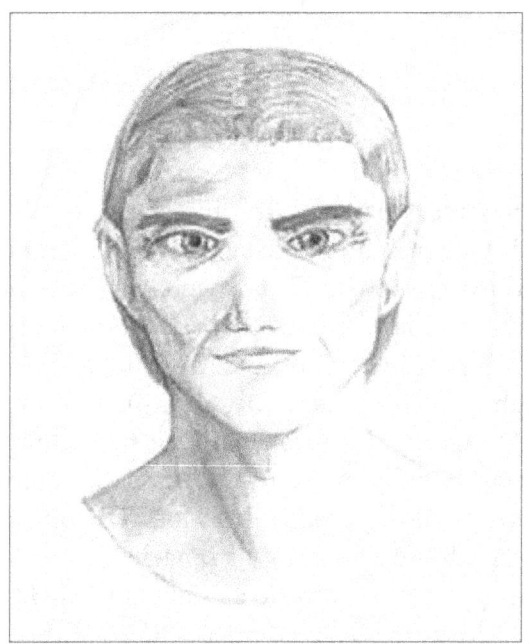

My Christmas angel.

CHAPTER 17

I Must Go Check on Him Now!

Early in my marriage, we frequently enjoyed holidays with my wife's brother and his wife in Ohio. During one such Memorial Day gathering, I found myself snoozing in a lawn chair with the summer flu while my brother-in-law, an excellent tradesman, completed yet another home improvement project. My wife and my sister-in-law took our daughter on a women-only shop-till-you-drop expedition to the mall. Thus, I took responsibility for watching my toddler, Mark, who slept blissfully in a playpen in the dining room.

Much to my work partner's irritation, I sought comfort from my throbbing headache and queasy stomach by snoozing in a chair. Strangely, I thought of the words to an old Contac cold remedy commercial jingle, which went, "A summer cold is a different animal…a different animal and ooh, for it hits you in the summer while you have lots to do!" I felt a bit guilty not helping. However, lethargic and hurting, my guilt did not rouse me to work, but I devised a helping strategy. I would nap under blue skies in the summer sunshine while listening to Cleveland's best oldies station. I rationalized, "At least I'm providing him a little company while making the most of a bad situation."

I snoozed for about an hour when, suddenly roused, I shot up and sat straight up in the chaise lounger. Fully awake, I exclaimed, "I must go check on Mark!"

My brother-in-law looked at me like I was crazy. He replied incredulously, "What do you have to do that for? He's in a playpen behind closed doors."

I got up and ran up the sloping backyard toward the house and yelled, "I have to check on him. I will be right back!" I sprinted to the house, bounding past the brick patio and onto the stairs. I almost ripped the door off its hinges, sprang into the house, and bounded through the recreation room into the kitchen. Looking through the kitchen doorway into the dining room, I found the playpen empty. I found the door leading outside wide open! My son, Mark, was gone. Scared, I faced every parent's worst nightmare and wondered if some pervert had kidnapped my son.

I raced from the dining room into the front yard. To my horror, Mark's little legs churned rapidly, taking him across the yard toward cars racing along East River Street. Fortunately, ten of his little steps equaled one of mine. In two bounds, I snatched him up well before he reached the road. Picking him up, I hugged him as tightly as I could. I couldn't be angry at my boy. Mark hadn't been disobedient. He didn't know what he was doing. I kissed my little boy and thanked God for His providential care.

My son had never climbed out of his playpen. Previously, he had never been able to open the dining room door. Had I been neglectful? How did I know to get up and run to the house?

Did Mark's guardian angel rouse me from my self-absorbed misery to save my son?

> For He will tell His angels to care for you in all
> his ways. (Ps 9:11, NLV)

CHAPTER **18**

Choose Life!

After I served four years as a chaplain at a major penitentiary, my employers asked me to move and help open a new prison. I accepted the offer, found a small apartment, and as summer waned, began a weekly commute from Terre Haute, Indiana, to a small town in southwestern Illinois. The roads from the two locations were excellent, and the drive took only two hours.

I returned home to be with my family on weekends but would return to my new job on Mondays. I awoke particularly early one summer morning, got ready for work, and got into my Plymouth Spirit for the trek to Illinois. I looked forward to bring a new institution online. Heading north on US 41, I turned on my oldies station and then headed west on I-70. I set the cruise control at sixty-five and settled in for the drive.

After crossing the Wabash River, I found my normal stations weren't playing anything I liked, and so I turned the radio off. I thought, *Less talk and more super oldies.* I sped past farmhouses amid the ripening Illinois cornfields. I passed Marshall, Illinois, knowing I would begin a long and boring stretch of road.

Apparently I dozed off. At one point during the ride, I heard a voice speak, "You sometimes think about death. Do you want to die? You aren't ready yet. We will take you now. You can come with us.

Do not fear. We will watch over your children. They will be all right. What do you choose?"

I found myself in a gray featureless setting. Confronted by an eerie voice with a bizarre message, I didn't know where I was or who was talking to me. Whoever or whatever offered the choices seemed to do so out of concern with no penalty to myself or to my children, but I felt uncomfortable. Something didn't ring true. The experience was like something out of Rod Serling's *The Twilight Zone*. I wondered if this was a trick to divide me from my family. I thought, *No one can love or raise my children as well as I can*. Confronted and choosing my fate, I replied, "I want to live!"

My eyes shot wide open. My car had drifted right and now hurtled along the very edge of I-70. The car sped precariously close to a steep embankment. Drowsy or asleep, I had not heard the warning grooves nor felt the car shake as my tires had passed over them. Perilously, the car sped poised to plummet down the grassy embankment to my certain death below. Calmly and slowly, I moved my vehicle back onto the interstate.

My heart burned like fire. Relieved, I thanked God for His providential care. I remembered the words found in Luke 24:32, which read, "They said to each other, did your heart not burn within us while he talked with us on the road and opened to us the Scriptures?" Today, many years later, I thank God for preserving me from death. I live comfortably, and my son and daughter are well adjusted and healthy. They lead successful lives. I like to think I may have had something to do with that. Proverbs 22:6 exhorts, "Train a child in the way that he or she shall go and when they are old they will not depart from it."

I sometimes muse about the voice that saved me from what could have easily been a fatal car crash. Who spoke to me? Where would they have taken me? Why wasn't I ready yet? Am I ready now? Are there certain things only I could fulfill as a loving parent?

An angel may have saved me. What a privilege to live and experience the opportunities God provides. I believe God provides a positive destiny for all his children. Perhaps I was not ready because I had not fulfilled all He wanted me to do. Had I chosen death, this would have been like committing suicide.

Sadly, some people choose suicide and death. Life is not always fair. Suicide seems a bitter fruit of negative outcomes in life. People may experience broken relationships, shattered dreams, and depression. Confronted by loss or loneliness, many feel the dreaded walls of failure enclose about them. Unfortunately, and erroneously, some see suicide as the only avenue of escape. There are solutions. Seek help!

Suicide seems to originate in Satanic deception. In John 8:44, Jesus tells us, "He was a murderer from the beginning, and abode not in truth, because there is not truth in him. When he speaks a lie, he speaks of his own; for he is a liar and the father of it." When a person is suicidal, perhaps Satan whispers in their ear and tells them there is no other way out of the problems which beset them. Satan seeks to overthrow a person's mind by dividing it against itself. As Jesus teaches in Mark 3:23–24, "If a kingdom is divided against itself, it cannot stand. And if a house is divided against itself, it cannot stand."(KJV, Public Domain)

Satan uses despair to divide a person against themselves. If you, my reader, are suicidal, choose life! Don't let the darkness close in around you. Reach out to others. See your doctor, your pastor, the chief of police, a loved one, or your supervisor—but get some help! Seek a way out of your problem.

> Look to the Lord and ask for His strength. Look
> to Him at all times. (I Chron. 16:11, NLV)

As Christ promises in Luke 11:9, "I tell you, ask and it will be given to you; seek and you will find; knock and it will be opened to you. For everyone who asks receives, and he who seeks finds, and to him that knocks it shall be opened." Ask for guidance and Christ will help you find it! Don't miss the opportunities in life God offers you. Please choose life!

> For He will tell His angels to care for you and keep
> all His ways. (Ps. 91:11, NLV)

CHAPTER 19

Look Behind You!

I drove home on US 40 with the speedometer set at fifty-five. My dad once told me, "Phil, it's important to look in the rearview mirror, and knowing what is going on behind you is as important as it is watching what is in front of you." Looking ahead, suddenly a voice advised, "Look behind you!" I glanced in my rearview mirror. A sedan hurtled at breakneck speed directly at my Nissan Rogue. The vehicle appeared quickly and as if from nowhere! In the front seat was a younger man, perhaps in his twenties, with long brown 1970s hippie-style hair. His wild determined eyes startled me.

His sedan rushed at over one hundred miles per hour directly on a collision course with my vehicle. My intuition told screamed, "*He isn't going to slow down! You're in danger!*" I wondered if someone had been sent to kill me. I didn't have time for fear. I sped up and moved quickly, steering well off the right of the road and stopping close a roadside pond's drainage ditch to avoid him.

Suddenly, his vehicle clipped my vehicle's left rear side anyway. He kept right, ongoing at over a hundred miles per hour! Stunned and in disbelief, I sat for a moment before carefully moving ahead to the next side road. I called 911 and reported the accident. I warned the state police of a young Caucasian male with long hair driving out of control in a white sedan headed north on US 40 toward exit 30 on

I-70. I told them it seemed likely he'd kill himself or, perhaps even worse, someone else!

After my 911 call, a man in a pick-up truck turned off of US 40 pulled up alongside of me and asked, "Did that car just hit you?"

I answered, "Yes. I did everything to get out of the way, and then he clipped me. He must have been going over a hundred! He didn't even stop after he hit me. I just called 911 and alerted the state police."

He replied, "Well, he just spun out at the intersection across from the Blue Springs Restaurant. He's stuck in the mud by the IDOT area. A guy in a truck stopped to watch him."

I thanked this kind man for his interest and drove directly to the intersection about a mile away. Sure enough, the same young man sat behind the steering wheel mired in a mud puddle up to his axles. He gunned the engine to get back on the road. Unable to effect his escape, he spun his wheels for a while then staggered from his car. Dressed in a T-shirt, shorts, and gym shoes yet impervious to the cold, he frantically sought to push his car from the mud. Heedless of the many bystanders that formed along the road, he tugged and pulled at the car. I wondered how anyone could be so drunk or what substance he was on. If Satan himself tried to kill me, Old Scratch couldn't have directed a more mindless two-thousand pound missile.

Grateful to be alive, I waited until the state police arrived on the scene and arrested him. Seething, I sat coldly, eyeing him from my vehicle. I angrily watched the wretch that hit my vehicle for many minutes. My anger turned to disgust then gave way to pity. I wondered what personal demons and problems troubled him. I saw a tormented, mindless, and witless beast.

My heart brightened, and I broke into a silly grin. I knew I was still alive and probably shouldn't have been. Spared once again, there is a bigger plan. I thought God has a purpose for me.

I hope this event woke the young man up and that he found his way in life. I've prayed for him. I'm grateful I survived to tell of God's miracles and mighty deeds.

For He will tell His angels to care for you and keep you in all His ways. (Ps. 91:11, NLV)

I will give thanks to the Lord with all my heart. I will tell of the great things you have done. (Ps. 9:1, NLV)

CHAPTER 20

Lincoln's Ghost?

It had been a long day. I unlocked my dormitory room at the seminary, quickly prepared for bed, slid between the cool sheets, adjusted my pillow, and immediately fell asleep. In the early morning hours, I felt drawn from my sleep. I awoke and looked across my room at my calendar. Instead of the monthly illustrations I'd grown used to, I saw a black silhouette of Abraham Lincoln's head looking from right to left. I wondered if the streetlight coming in through the windowpane played tricks on my eyes. I shook my head from side to side. Now completely awake, I stared in disbelief, but the shade remained clear and sharp. It did not speak. In time, I fell back asleep.

Lincoln's ghost.

The next morning, I considered what Mr. Lincoln's silhouette meant. Why appear to an insignificant person? Why would a nobody rate a visit from one of America's greatest presidents? I dressed, then walked across the street to the dining hall. I picked up a discarded newspaper and went to the special features. Amazingly as if beyond coincidence, the date was April 14, the anniversary of President Abraham Lincoln's Good Friday Assassination. The article chronicled the terrible events of Lincoln's murder at the hands of John Wilkes Booth at Ford's Theater in 1865. I wondered why Lincoln's silhouette would appear to me on the anniversary of the event. Mr. Lincoln's apparition appeared at the time he would lay dying in a rooming house across from the theater. Busy living my life, I soon forgot about Lincoln's visitation.

At the time, I served as an intern at the primarily ethnically Black Church of the Good Shepherd, at 57th and Prairie on the south side of Chicago. My duties included visiting the sick and the shut-in along Michigan Avenue. Poor and not owning a vehicle, I took the bus or walked. As one of the only White faces visiting in the neighborhood, I soon began to understand what it was like to be a minority. My visits occasioned stares of disbelief and an occasional racial epithet. But, by in large, people in the neighborhood ignored me or treated me kindly. After all, I wasn't changing the world, but I did learn a lot from my mentor, Dr. Kenneth B. Smith, President of the Urban League.

Many years later, following the death of my grandfather, I thought I understood why Lincoln's silhouette appeared to me that night. My father inherited a picture of Mr. Lincoln, presented to my grandfather by the Illinois Secretary of State, Charles S. Carpentier. When I asked my father for the picture, he graciously gave it to me. The picture remains a prized possession. The picture enjoyed a special place of honor in my home.

Others have reported seeing Mr. Lincoln's restless spirit. Grace Coolidge, the wife of President Calvin Coolidge, reportedly saw Lincoln looking out of a White House window. While visiting FDR, Queen Wilhelmina of the Netherlands told the president she saw Lincoln's ghost in the Lincoln bedroom. Teddy Roosevelt, Eleanor

Roosevelt, and Jackie Kennedy all reported sensing his presence. President Truman stated some household staff reported seeing Mr. Lincoln during his presidential tenure.

After viewing his silhouette, I read several Lincoln biographies. Numerous works record Mrs. Lincoln's interest in the paranormal. Additionally, historians report Lincoln told his wife and two personal friends about a precognitive dream which foretold his death.

Mr. Lincoln may be a restless spirit. However, I think the president's appearances may be seen as more than just repeat hauntings of a man who died suddenly in a violent circumstance. Now, over forty-five years later, I think President Lincoln's appearance meant more. I interpret his appearances to mean that his work is not done in America. America, the great melting pot, remains the hope of immigrants from around the world. As a people, Americans must try to live up to our Constitutional guarantee of providing equal opportunity to all races. Our nation continues to make progress, but we are not there! The Great Emancipator's life remains a model, exhorting us to be the nation described in the Declaration of Independence and Bill of Rights.

CHAPTER 21

Behold, I Make All Things New!

Senator Everett M. Dirksen

My supervisors sent me to assist with official business at Pekin, Illinois. Honored to help, I traveled northward on Interstate 55 to Illinois 9, west to my motel. Nearing my destination, signs near Glendale Memorial Gardens alert travelers to the Senator Everett M. Dirksen gravesite. Senator Dirksen's gravesite interested me. As a young man, I enjoyed the honor of serving as a US Senate Page under Senator Dirksen's patronage. I wept at his funeral service held at the National Cathedral.

Upon my arrival at the motel, I found a counterpart had yet to arrive. With time on my hands, I drove back to the cemetery to pay my respects. Once a legend in Washington, and a favorite on the American political scene, I expected to find a great monument to the senator. However, humble in life, the good Senator desired no great monument upon his death. There weren't any signs directing visitors to the Senator's grave. Unable to find it, I left disappointed; I couldn't pay my proper respects.

Humble Bronze Head Marker

Many years later, I learned Senator Dirksen chose a small bronze marker which might easily be overlooked. As one of God's servants and a spiritual man, it seemed he chose a humble grave. Nevertheless, Senator Dirksen would not be overlooked or forgotten by American history, which bestowed many accolades and tributes in his honor.

After returning to the motel, I asked the receptionist if my partner had arrived. Wondering if something might be wrong and before checking in, I asked to see my room. The desk attendant provided a key, and I went upstairs to appraise the room. Sensing something wasn't right, and somehow confident the other member of the team wasn't coming, I exited the room and walked down the hallway.

Then I saw him! Senator Dirksen no longer appeared old and gnarled or sporting those famous big bags under his eyes. No longer scarred by the ravages of time or the stresses of power, Dirksen stood translucent. No longer dressed in crumpled clothes with an old belt hitched haphazardly over a large belly, he wore a neatly pressed gray suit, white shirt, and dark tie. His face appeared middle aged and without wrinkles. Cocking his head to the side, with eyes twinkling as if to figure out who I was, he beamed with genuine joy. Spellbound and removed from space and time, I returned his gaze. He turned, looked back over his shoulder, eyes still sparkling with lips smiling, and disappeared.

Stunned, I slowly returned from a celestial time and the power of the senator's apparition. I walked downstairs to the front desk. I called the prison only to discover the program review postponed. The appropriate authority failed to notify our chain of command. Afterward, I wondered if his appearance might be a courtesy to someone who sought his grave to pay their respects. I imagined there might be fewer individuals visiting his graveside thirty years after his death. I mused that during the peak of his power, many desired his company. Friends, family, and others leave us as the years pass.

I reflected on the Senator's visit Mr. Dirksen appeared to me in the prime of his life. No longer aged but immortal, Dirksen had put on the imperishable. Senator Everett M. Dirksen supported and aided the Civil Rights Act of 1964.

In March of 1966, he introduced a constitutional amendment to permit public school administrators to allow organized prayers in public schools. His apparition reminded me a purpose exists beyond mankind's immediate experience. We face old age and infinity, yet as we transit from this world's cares, there is healing. Those possessing temporal power or vast wealth use it wisely in pursuit of God's kingdom. Faithful leaders walk the golden pathway.

> Death must be distinguished from dying, with which it is often confused. (Sydney Smith)

> For if a man belongs to Christ he is a new person. His old life is gone. New life has begun. (I Cor. 5:17, NLV)

> O death, where is your power? O death, where are your pains? The pain in death is sin. Sin has power over those in the law. But God is the One who gives us power over sin through Jesus Christ Our Lord. (I cor 15:55, NLV)

> Then the One sitting on the throne said, "See I make all things new! (Rev. 21:5, NLV)

CHAPTER 22

President Lincoln and Senator Dirksen—Co-laborers in God's Vineyard

Over the years, I became aware that President Lincoln's and Senator Dirksen's apparitions seemed to be linked. The Lord God Almighty provided these two political heavyweights' special missions to establish greater racial equality in the United States. Coworkers in God's vineyard, they "toiled in the heat of the day," changing America's political landscape.

Given their physical appearance and the times in which they were set, initially one might not see the similarities between the two men. Yet these two Illinoisans share numerous similarities. Both men rose to national prominence from humble backgrounds. Both, reared on farms, worked for small businesses until aspiring to local elective offices. Both passed the Illinois bar before going to Washington. Both left elected office, achieving national prominence as leaders of the Republican Party. Both died at the height of their power. Mr. Lincoln served as president of the United States from January 1861 until his death in Washington, DC., on April 15, 1865. Mr. Dirksen, the man from Pekin, served as the minority leader of the United States Senate from 1959 until his death in Washington, DC., on September 7, 1969.

Everett M. Dirksen painting. Artist: Richard Hood Harryman, 1984. United States Senate Gallery (Public Domain).	Everett M. Dirksen bronze statue. Sculptor: Carlo Tolpo, 1975. Courtesy Pekin, Illinois Park District (Public Domain).

These icons, separated by a century, remain synonymous with major milestones furthering racial equality in America. President Lincoln, leader of the Republican Party, signed the Emancipation Proclamation in 1863 and ensured the end of slavery. Historians note although the northern states won the war, the southern states won reconstruction with the establishment of Jim Crow laws. Senator Everett M. Dirksen, like President Lincoln before him, also enlisted in the cause of racial equality.

In the early 1960s, Rev. Martin Luther King Jr. sounded a clarion call for racial justice but needed political allies to pursue his dream. Rev. King brought a million people to the Capitol Mall, but it would take people accustomed to the halls of power in the Capitol Building to affect his dream. President Lyndon B. Johnson supported the Voting Rights Act of 1964, but only his old colleague and Republican Senate leader Everett M. Dirksen could engineer the bill's passage. Like Lincoln before him, compelled by the great movement of his time, Dirksen would champion minority rights.

The senator rose to the occasion, and, as a true champion, brought victory. Senator Dirksen used all his experience, power, and political acumen, bringing passage. Thus, the two coworkers in God's vineyard, President Lincoln and Senator Dirksen, battled for racial justice and served God's righteous will.

Upon the vote to cloture on the filibuster targeting the Civil Rights Act of 1964, Dirksen quoted Victor Hugo, stating, "Stronger than all the armies is an idea whose time has come." Senator Dirksen added, "The time has come for equality of opportunity in sharing of government, in education, and in employment. It must not be stayed or denied."

Co-workers in God's kingdom: Senator Everett Dirksen
and President Abraham Lincoln (personal property
of author). Photo by Philip W. Chapman.

Abraham Lincoln and Everett Dirksen provide shining examples of faithful people called by God to effect change. These two humble men of character, destined to fill seats of power, witnessed the hand of God moving in America's affairs. Lincoln and Dirksen provided a political legacy undimmed by death. Both lie in the soil of their beloved state of Illinois. Their actions helped clear the way for greater racial equality in America and eventually for the election of the first American president of African American descent. Co-laborers in the vineyard, their work is not yet finished in America or across the globe.

> I Cor. 3:7-9: "This shows that the one who plants or the one that waters is not the important one. God is the important one. He makes it grow. The one who plants and the one who waters is alike. Each one will get his own pay. For we work together with God." (NLV)

> Whoever wants to be great among you must be the one who is owned and cares for all. For the Son of Man did not come to be cared for. He came to care for others. He came to give His life so many could be bought with His blood and be made free from sin. (Mark 10: 43-45, NLV)

CHAPTER 23

The Wind Blows Where It Will

As my father-in-law lay slowly wasting away from cancer in Florida, my wife—a nurse—went to care for him. A strong, self-reliant man, he lay unable to accomplish the smallest of tasks. Sadly, at the end, his spirit gone, he seemed totally debilitated. She was there for him. Given his misery and suffering, his passing seemed a blessing.

I worked toward my Master's degree at Fort Jackson, South Carolina. I sometimes grew tired of my books and stayed in shape doing belly crunchers, push-ups, sit-ups, and jogging. I loved long jogs. One sultry warm morning, I left the housing area and jogged along the Fort Jackson golf course. The sun blazed overhead. Nevertheless, I enjoyed this route, as it afforded a panorama of lush green rolling hills and beautiful pine trees. Downcast, I missed my pregnant wife and tiny strawberry blonde daughter. I sadly mused at my father-in-law's fate. Downcast, I did an "airborne shuffle" pace for about seven miles. There was no wind on that humid, hot day. Before the days of shirts with wicking, I jogged, drenched with sweat, with my wet T-shirt pasted to my body.

I headed for home and turned into the housing area, rounded a corner, and gazed longingly at our familiar backyard. Azaleas we'd planted stood at the foot of the giant pine trees behind the house. I looked forward to a refreshing drink of water. Finally, now at the end of my jog, I looked up to the blue sunlit sky and began my "cool-off walk." Thinking of my father-in-law, I prayed, "Lord, if there is life after death, please give me a little sign." A strong breeze suddenly sprang up, and the pine boughs behind our home began to move and rustle. A soothing whisper moved through the pine branches. The breeze lasted for about thirty seconds then left as quickly as it had appeared. I witnessed the only breeze all day. Some might call this a weird coincidence.

However, that wind wasn't a coincidence. Clearly the Lord sent me an answer.

Jesus teaches in John 3:8; "The wind blows where it wants to you hear it's sound. You do not know where it comes or where it goes. It is the same with everyone who is born of the spirit." (NLV)

In John 14:1-2, Jesus provides words of encouragement, "Do not let you hearts be troubled. . You have put your trust in me. There are many rooms in my Father's house." (NLV)

In First Corinthians 15:58 the Apostle Paul exhorts believers; "So then Christian brothers be strong. Do not allow anyone to change your mind. Always do your work in the Lord. You know whatever you do for Him will not be wasted." (NLV)

CHAPTER 24

You Reap What You Sow

The sun, low in the late-evening sky, cast shadows across the road as I headed home south on IL 143. Just north of the I-70, I approached a bridge spanning a small stream bracketed by steel guardrails on each side. Tall trees dug their roots deeply into the stream's wet bank concealed by underbrush. The stream proved a thoroughfare for wildlife. Here, man and wildlife often meet unexpectedly with raccoon, possums, skunks, squirrels, and turtles always getting the worst of the exchange.

When I see lifeless, bloodied bodies of animals left to rot on the road, I whisper, "May God rest your soul." When it proves safe to do so, I brake for animals. I even slow down to prevent butterflies from being plastered to my car's grill. I honor life.

As I entered the two lane confines of the small bridge, a young whitetail buck hopped the guardrail, onto the right lane, and directly in front of my subcompact Pontiac G6. I could not avoid the animal and enjoyed no time for a complete stop. The deer, apparently not understanding its peril, stood motionlessly gazing at my rapid approach. I pumped the brakes twice and then braced for the inevitable accident.

As the young beast's eyes locked with mine, I thought of the word *Cernunnos*. The deer looked quizzically at me through the windshield. I hit the deer head-on after pumping the brakes for the second time. The buck went airborne sideways, its hooves, underbelly, neck, snout, and head facing me. Fortunately, instead of flying up and over the hood and killing me instantly, the animal flew windshield high in front of the car's hood.

As if choreographed by some unseen force, my car engine stopped. The buck, still in midair, miraculously decelerated at exactly the same pace as my car. The young spitter hit the pavement in the middle of my lane and slid to a stop directly in front of my vehicle. Amazed, I exited the vehicle. My engine was totaled, but the deer got the worst of it. I approached quietly and gently whispered, "I'm sorry." The broken creature looked at me, grunted once, and died.

Upon arriving home, I told a neighbor. She told me that some twenty years before, a high school teen had been killed in exactly the same place while returning from a movie in Edwardsville, Illinois. Sadly, the teen's car hit a doe which flew up over the hood and crashed through the windshield, killing them. Following some research, I suggested a yellow deer-warning sign be placed before the bridge. According to government experts, this was unnecessary because the rules governing the placement of deer signs didn't apply. Make sense to you?

Afterward, I looked up and found the name *Cernunnos*. In multiple sources, he's known as the Horned One; I found the ancient Celts worshiped Cernunnos as Lord of Wild Things. Could it be that be that due to my concern for sparing wild beasts and my prayers for their dead bodies, I had been protected by God?

> A man who is right with God cares for the animal, but the sinful man has no pity. (Proverbs 12:10, NLV)

> If you throw your bread upon the water you find it after many days. (Ecclsiastes 11:1, NLV)

I care about animals. Therefore, perhaps I reaped what I'd sown. Ecclesiastes 11:1 teaches, "Cast your bread upon the water and it will come back to you." As the old saying goes, "What goes around comes around."

CHAPTER 25

More than They Bargained For

I was honored to serve as a chaplain at the correctional brigade at Fort Riley, Kansas. Early one morning, I arrived at the auxiliary chapel to find three young troopers waiting for me.

Each explained they needed to see me immediately. I met with each individually and listened intently to their experience the night before. Each described a frightening occult experience. A Wiccan soldier with artistic talents drew a Ouija board and invited three of his friends to a séance. They snuck off to a deserted WWII barracks to contact the spirits but got more than they bargained for!

The young soldiers explained the Ouija board ceremony had proceeded harmlessly until one of the three participants asked questions no one else in the room could know. The board then began to provide them with answers to these questions, revealing their exact social security numbers and the names of deceased family members. The soldiers reported sensing a terrible presence using the board that asked them to engage in sexual activity. The soldiers all ran from the scene.

One Catholic soldier said he knew better than to participate in the ritual, but he thought nothing would happen. He said he'd never do it again and said he now knew why it was wrong. We prayed together for his deliverance from the entity he'd encountered. The second soldier reported feeling demon-possessed. Scared, he said he suffered headaches and insomnia. I provided him with counseling and encouragement for many weeks. I did some research and provided him with ancient Christian prayers for deliverance from the demon. The third, afraid but seemingly less affected than the other two, asked only for prayer.

The fourth soldier had talked the other three into something they thought might be a joke yet might prove interesting and enjoyable. The three got more than they had bargained for. All four started attending church, and two accepted Jesus Christ as their personal Lord and Savior. I encouraged the third and baptized a Catholic, not only to attend my services but to attend confession and return to mass. In time, all three returned to normalcy, but each learned from the harrowing occult experience. This fourth man, a Wiccan, said he respected how I was helping the other three but would not convert to Christianity.

I reported to the battalion commander and suggested the Ouija board be burned. The soldier agreed. The commander took and destroyed the Ouija board. The soldiers experienced the dangers of occult practices.

> Let no one among you consult with a charmer, or a consulter with familiar spirits, or a wizard, or a necromancer. (Deut. 18:11, KJV, Public Domain)

> And there was in their synagogue a man with an unclean spiritand he cried out saying;" let us alone Jesus of Nazareth. Art Thou come to destroy us? I know thee, who Thou art, the Holy One of God. And Jesus rebuked him saying, hold thy peace, and come out of him. (Mark 1:23-26, KJV, Public Domain)

THE US CORRECTIONAL BRIGADE is closed. However, did the four soldiers open a spiritual portal that still exists? If so, do spirits linger?

26

An Unwanted Visitor

Although I've been blessed with miracles and positive otherworldly experiences, the second sight is not without peril and may bring unwanted visitors. The following story of a shadow mass describes a case in point.

Home alone, I finished my early afternoon lunch, washed off my plate, and sauntered from the kitchen toward my favorite chair in the living room to watch TV. I stopped dead in my tracks when, to my astonishment, my gaze focused on a black mist. I'd never seen a cloud quite like it. Aghast, I eyed the dark aura warily. Content to observe it, I made no effort to speak or to move further toward it. Instinctively, I understood the dark entity remained the predator, and I existed as prey. My gut told me this negative entity harbored a deep intentional malice.

A cruel low, guttural voice spoke from the center of a dark mist, "I have Sherry here." I hadn't seen my sister in decades. Estranged, we'd pursued different lifestyles. Sherry had suffered a long kidney ailment and recently passed in a Chicago hospital alone and surrounded by strangers. She'd hid this ailment from the family. Once a heavy, full-bodied woman, she'd eventually wasted away to almost nothing.

I quickly considered what this foul creature's words meant. I concluded this wicked creature now used Sherry as bait to lure me. I found myself confronted by an evil and powerful adversary. It sought to feed on me and to delight in my misery! I would not enter into the dark mass. I silently held my ground. Then words of command came to me from an unknown source. "In the name of Christ, I command you to leave this place. Go to the abyss prepared for you from the beginning of time for the devil and his angels. Be gone! Go!" The dark cloud disappeared.

Afterward, as if waking from a dream, I returned to the light of summer's day streaming through my home's windows. I worried for my sister but didn't dwell on it. Eternal consequences follow the choices we make in this life. I have prayed for her soul and the souls of those who drove her to a life of ruin.

> I do not ask you take them out of the world. I ask you keep them from the devil. (John 17:15, NLV)

> They said; Put your trust in the Lord Jesus Christ, and you and your family will be saved from punishment of sin. (Acts 16:31, NLV)

I pray every meal that Sherry's soul may be released from the evil spirit's control. I pray regularly for the eternal repose of my sister's soul.

CHAPTER 27

Warning—Dangers of the Occult

Given the previous story of the soldiers' experiences at the correctional brigade and my personal confrontation with a shadow, I provide the following checklist which should help you in determining if a supernatural experience may be dangerous. Writers and psychic investigators report the following experiences remain a cause of concern. If you are involved in the occult, consider the following warning signals.

1. The experience leads to a feeling of terror or dread.
2. You begin to hear knocks, scratches, or see menacing or dark forms in your home.
3. You or others notice or experience negative changes in your or someone else's personality.
4. You or another becomes withdrawn or mean toward those they care about.
5. You or a significant other begins to speak in unknown languages, perhaps growls like a predator!
6. You hear voices that tell you to hurt others.
7. You become depressed or preoccupied with death, sad music, and make plans to hurt yourself.

WARNING

If you experience these signs please seek assistance from a quali-fied clergy or a licensed psychologist. Don't wait! Be strong. Act now because you could be in danger!

> Jesus prayed; "I do not ask you take them out of the world. I ask you keep them from the devil." (John 17: 15, NLV)

CHAPTER 28

Dream of Warning? The Capitol Building

Shortly following 9/11, I dreamed I stood on the Capitol Mall in Washington, DC. I saw the Capitol building. A huge silver plane (Boeing 757) with no distinguishing markings flew over the Library of Congress, with its nose down headed directly toward the Capitol Building. I woke up before it actually crashed into the Capitol building.

The Capitol building.

I provide the following possible interpretations for this waking dream:

1. The plane, which the passengers purposefully crashed into a Pennsylvania field, was headed to the Capitol building. The would-be assassins intended to use the mall as their approach path and crash the plane directly into the base of the Capitol building rotunda.

2. However, my waking dream could also be symbolic. Since the plane had no markings, it may have meant Al-Qaeda hopes to destroy American interests from the air. Their first choice may be a commercial airliner's because this will accomplish two objectives simultaneously. If the Capitol building is a primary target, the first objective is to destroy an important American icon and to disrupt the American political process. The second and simultaneous objective is to destroy the American tourist industry by convincing people it's unsafe to fly.

However, if they fail to hijack the commercial plane, perhaps their fallback plan could be to use a cargo airliner. If they were able to enlist the help of a radical employed in the international cargo industry, they might fly under security's radar and hit what they missed the first time.

3. Simultaneous attack.

Given their desire to destroy an American icon, if their dream for an air attack, fails they may opt for other means on the ground during a simultaneous attack. For example, terrorists might choose to attack the subway while trying to take over a portion of a congressional office building. To effect a breach in a congressional office building, terrorists might use a suicide bomber to blow out a door where burly security guards are stationed and then send in a commando team to control a selected office, entire corridor, or a committee room.

With sufficient resources, Al-Qaeda or Muslim radicals execute a synchronous attack on America's Capitol complex. Such a plan might utilize a suicide bomber with a brief case or backpack to detonate on the subway at the Smithsonian or at the Congressional office building terminal. The subway attack could be synchronous with an attack designed to commandeer a portion of a Congressional office building. It appears Washington, DC, continues to be a target. The foiled attempts at Heathrow Airport, the attempt over the Atlantic Ocean by Shoe Bomber Reid, or the foiled plot over the Pacific called Bojinka are not the end of air terror.

CHAPTER 29

An Eagle's Call

Glad to be up north in Wisconsin, I awoke in the dark stillness of our cabin before dawn. I dressed quietly and donned my jeans, sweat-shirt, low-cut hiking boots and adjusted my ball cap squarely on my head. I moved silently to the pier as the night's breezes serenaded the sound sleepers I left behind.

I opened the door and peered into the darkness toward the lake. No stars; only blackness greeted me. It didn't matter. I knew my path and strode confidently to the shore and a wooden pier. The pine needles crunched softly beneath my feet. Waves murmured, lapping against the shore. The dock faced east to the coming sunrise. Finally, I reached the land of in-between, where God dwells. I sought love of the Creator reflected in His creation.

Alone? Seated comfortably in a plastic chair on the dock, I closed my eyes and began meditating in the dark. The whisper of gentle waves receded as I breathed steadily in cadence. I inhaled four counts, thinking, *Yahweh*, and exhaled four counts, thinking the word *evil*. Seated in the blackness, I left the world behind.

I stayed focused on the one who makes things happen. Meditating and surrounded by the immensity of creation, I lost track of time. A harbinger of dawn arrived. The birds raised their morning carols to declare their Maker's praise. Perhaps entranced, I opened my eyes. In time, the land grew fully lit as a hidden sun rose above the horizon. The night's darkness receded, revealing a canopy of low-hanging clouds and swirling mists dancing on the lake's surface.

I lingered, the wind etched an ever-changing pattern of waves. Abruptly, suddenly, the clouds parted, as if by some invisible force, providing a window which revealed a blinding silver sun. To my amazement, a screeching bald eagle, with wings outstretched on the wind, burst through this portal. Riding gusting winds above the lake, my visitor circled tightly below the low-flying clouds. My guest's white head and tail, accented by its dark body, gleamed in the sun's powerful beams. Cocking its head, this caller wheeled and swooped down directly toward me. Perhaps thirty yards away, my raptor halted and extended its wings then banked sharply upward, disappearing into the mist.

Isaiah 40:31 "But those who hope in the Lord will renew their strength. They will soar on wings like eagles, they will run and not be weary, they will walk and not be faint." (KJV, Public Domain)
Photo Credit: USFW George Gentry, Public Domain, FWS.gov

A bald eagle remains a powerful totem to Native American tribes. I later asked a Lakota medicine man what the eagle's appearance might mean. He replied, "*Wakinyan thanka*"—pronounced

Wakan Tonkan (Great Spirit or Great Mystery)—"wanted you to know how powerful he is."

The Old and New Testaments emphasize the importance of seeking God. In Mark, Jesus provides an example of rising a great while before day in the great outdoors to commune with His heavenly Father. As Psalm 19 suggests, I believe Christ found God's love and word reflected in nature. Consider the scriptures provided below. Do they speak to you? Do they call you to try something new?

> Look for the Lord while He may be found. Call upon Him while He is near. (Isaiah 55:6, NLV)

> In the morning, before the sun was up Jesus went to a place where He could be alone. He prayed there. (Mark 1:35, NLV)

> The heavens are telling the greatness of, and the great open spacesabove show the works of His hands. (Psalm 19:1, NLV)

CHAPTER 30

A Celestial Dance: The Music of the Spheres

A diverse group of males and females (young and old) dressed in variety of fashions from sports coats with button down shirts and slacks, bell bottoms, tie-dyed shirts with sandals, to shorts, tee shirts, and gym shoes, entered the classroom, and took their seats. Our professor, clean-shaven with a button-down shirt, pressed slacks, and shiny loafers, arrived. He stood behind the podium and announced, "Today you will do something different in class. You will get in touch with the holy! You can't talk about what you don't experience. Today we'll meditate."

I invite each of you to get comfortable, relax, and use your own technique get in touch with God. My mind went to the old song entitled, "Turn Your Radio On Get in Touch With God," then smiled. I believe a person with faith coupled with meditation technique, much like a person at a radio, can dial in a message from thin air. The professor wasted no further time, and after a brief minute's interlude, we began.

The professor intoned, "Close your eyes and begin." I hoped to cleanse myself and enter God's presence. I chose a simple breathing mantra meditation. I started by breathing in for four counts and then exhaling for four counts. I relaxed my body, starting with my toes, and then moved through my feet, legs, pelvis, torso, chest, and neck to the top of my head.

After relaxing, I started my mantra, saying (thinking) the name *Yahweh* as I breathed in for four counts, then thought the word *evil* while exhaling four counts. I asked God to enter my heart and purge all evil.

One of my professors, an existential phenomenologist, used to refer to a person's innermost moving. The ancient Jews believed the heart is greater than the sum of it's parts. These parts included thought, emotions, volition, and determine an individual's personality. The ancient Greeks believed in a soul as a conscious spirit with the ability to reason. The Greek word *psyche* comes from the ancient root synonymous with *breath*. My mantra, using breathing, allows a person to surrender to Yahweh and invites God to enter into the heart or soul of a person.

After getting into the zone, I lost track of time. Transported to a cosmic realm, I found myself visiting an alternative reality. A surreal dimension surrounded me, lit by a diffused light; it held no worldly things with which to orient myself. I gained a new perspective made possible by the one who makes things happen.

I imagined floating mysteriously in a surreal dimension fed by wellsprings of an invisible cosmic wind. I wasn't alone. Not far from me, others shared this element. Middle-aged and younger people smiled, laughed, and danced in a circle. They shared a celestial dance, seemingly aware of a harmony I could not hear but whose joyful strains beckoned me. I now believe the music of the spheres remains a vast symphony celebrating God's love and creation. I wanted to join them.

The professor's voice interrupted us. He called, "It's time to come back. Come back slowly."

I replied, "I don't want to come back. I'm in a beautiful place."

Insistent, he repeated, "You must come back. We don't want to lose you."

Reluctantly, I returned to class. The Holy Spirit had revealed to me the creative power of God and the music of the spheres.

We may move in different circles, but we dance the same dance on the music of the spheres. (Wald Wasserman)

The fanatical atheists are like slaves who are still feeling the weight of their chains which they have thrown off after hard struggle. They are like creatures who, in their grudge against traditional religion as "the opium of the masses," cannot hear the music of the spheres. (Albert Einstein)

The heavenly spheres make music for us. The holy twelve dance with us. All things join in the dance! Ye who dance not, know not what we are knowing. (Gustav Holst)

CHAPTER **31**

Meditation

Find a place without distraction that you like. Perhaps use a chapel or the great outdoors.

Seat yourself comfortably and close your eyes.

Breathe in for four counts.

Exhale for four counts.

Establish a cadence.

Depending upon your faith, while inhaling for the first four counts, think of one of the following names: *Yahweh* or *Jesus*.

While exhaling for four counts, think of the word *evil*.

Continue for ten minutes or more.

This meditation may allow the Holy Spirit to fill your heart and touch your innermost movings.

Joggers may easily adapt this meditation for use outside or inside on a treadmill.

If running outside, focus your eyes on a point in front of you. Begin your jog.

Inhale for four steps, thinking the name Yahweh or Jesus. Exhale for four steps, thinking of the word *evil*. Continue your meditation until your jog is over.

Note: meditation is not magic [magick]. Meditation is more than a proper technique of appropriate posture or pronouncing deities' names correctly. Sincere belief in God and a desire to submit to

God's will may bring results. Sincerely seek God, and He will communicate with you.

> The best things in life are simple. Simple things work. They don't foul up. (Lois Duncan)

> Then he went away by Himself to pray in the desert. (Luke 5:16, NLV)

> Ask, and what you are asking for will be given you. Look, and what you are looking for you will find. Everyone who asks receives what he asks for. (Mt. 7:7, NLV)

CHAPTER 32

Coincidence or the Power of Prayer?

During my teenage years, we got the news Grandpa and Grandma would celebrate their fiftieth wedding anniversary up north in Land O' Lakes, Wisconsin. I couldn't contain my excitement! What news! As a little boy, we'd spent summers at Big Portage Lake. I recall its blue sparkling waves always seemed to shine brightly in a summer breeze. I'd watched black-feathered bald eagles with their white heads and tails soaring overhead. Warm summer days of joy brought speed boats skimming across shimmering silver waters. The boats' young water skiers always smiled and waved to us. Glorious days might be followed by cool, crisp evenings spent around campfires cooking hot dogs and marshmallows. Big Portage Lake, my childhood paradise.

My grandparents' humble summer cottage remains in my mind's eye and is still home to some of my happiest childhood memories. I hold golden remembrances of fishing for Walleye, Smallmouth Bass, or Jumbo Perch, jumping into crystal clear waters from the end of the dock and loving the evening campfires on our sandy little beach. We didn't have indoor plumbing until the late 1950s, and so the white outhouse with green trimming sat out back. We weren't rich and had to watch our pennies, but we were wealthy in ways the magnificent beauty and wholesome activities nature afforded. To return and see Gramps and Grams, all the cousins, aunts, and uncles seemed a magical dream come true.

There was only one problem; Northern Wisconsin's August tended to be very rainy. Gray stratus clouds might come for days on end. These rains refreshed the spring-fed lakes and many streams but unfortunately could put a damper on our many activities. Therefore, as we finished packing the car and set out, I quietly asked for the impossible. I prayed, "Please send us sunny weather for our vacation."

So as we reached Wisconsin and drove northward toward Land O' Lakes, the skies grew gray, and then it began to steadily rain. I resigned myself that it appeared to be God's will that we endure storms. Still, I thought hopefully, *It may clear up after we've been there a few days.* Crowded together, we continued on in our car, listening to the radio and counting the cows and horses of America's Dairyland. Yesteryear's loud windshield wipers flapped back and forth to the sound of the falling rain.

After what seemed like an eternity, we reached the outskirts of Land O' Lakes and turned off of US 45 onto County B, heading west. The rain slowed a bit. We headed for the Voight's old place our dad arranged to rent for this special occasion. The Voight's cottage stood just two doors down from our grandparents' place. As our car moved onto Big Portage Lake Road, the rain slackened a bit more. We turned onto the Voight's sand driveway and parked behind the cottage. As we opened the car's doors, the rain stopped completely. Wow! I thought, *Maybe we'll have great weather after all!*

We did! Not soon after we unpacked, the low-hanging rain-laden clouds disappeared, not to return. As we swam, fished, barbecued, water skied, or went out to dinner, nothing but blue skies or puffy white cumulus clouds greeted us. Family and many friends coming from all over the US attended an enormous banquet at the Gateway Inn. Everyone celebrated fifty years of a successful marriage. The local newspaper reported our gala reception was a resounding success. Afterward, some family lingered to benefit from uncommonly good weather.

Finally, the moment I dreaded came and our grand family vacation came to an end. Sadly, there would never be another like it. We awoke early on a gray morning, wanting to gain a good start for the long, inevitable drive home. After packing the car, we crammed ourselves inside, then the last car door slammed. Suddenly, as if on cue, light raindrops fell. A steady rain greeted us on County Road B. God spoke to me that day. I believed God answered my prayer.

I never told anyone in my family. It remained my and the Lord's secret. I once told my friend's dad, Maynard. He asked incredulously, "You think God changed the weather for your vacation?"

I replied without hesitation, "Yes, of course! What else could it be? Coincidence?"

Later, I strayed from the innocence of my youth. I sometimes forgot to pray, read Scripture, show kindness, ask the Lord's guidance, or act accordingly to God's commands. Nevertheless, one summer, over fifty years ago, God answered a boy's prayer. Now as I grow old, I remember a glorious summer up north. I didn't know how blessed we were. Thank you, Lord. Those were some of the best days of our lives.

> Then you will call upon ME and come to pray to ME, and I will listen to you. (Jeremiah 29:12, NLV)

> All things you ask in prayer, you will recieve if you have faith. (Mt. 21:22, NLV)

BIBLIOGRAPHY

Abraham Lincoln. Wikipedia, 2023. http://en.wikipedia.org/wiki/Abraham_Lincoln.

Badcock, Maltbie Davenport. "This Is My Father's World." Tune Terra Beata. Published in 306 Hymnals, 1901. Public Domain. Hymnary.org.

Biographical Directory of the United States Congress. 1774–Present. http://bioguide.congress.gov/scriptsbiodisplay.pl?index=d000360.

Bogan, Eric C. "The Dangers of the Occult." Burton, Michigan. Accessed July 17, 2022. http://www.hmclive.org.

Burnham, Sophy. *A Book of Angels.* New York: Random House, 1990.

Catton, Bruce. *This Hallowed Ground.* Garden City, New York: Doubleday and Company, 1956.

Dirksen, Everett M. "Supporting Cloture on the United States Senate Civil Rights Bill." June 14, 1964. Senate Historical Office, 2023. Public Domain. https//www.senategov: Speeches, Dirksen, Civil Rights.

"Gettysburg Address." Today in History–November 19. Library of Congress (gov), 2023. Public Domain. http://encarta.msn.com/encyclopedia_761563946/Gettysburg_Address.html.

Goodrich, Thomas. *The Darkest Dawn.* Indianapolis: Indiana University Press, 2005.

Gualzo, Allen C. *Lincoln's Emancipation Proclamation: The End of Slavery in America.* New York: Simon and Schuster, 2004.

Hine, Stuart K. "How Great Thou Art."

Jung, Carl G. *Synchronicity: An Acausal Connecting Principle.* (New Jersey: Princeton University Press, 1973.

Lamon, Ward Hill. *Recollections of Abraham Lincoln 1847–1865.* University of Nebraska Press, 1994).

Lincoln Assassination. Accessed 2007. http://aol.com/RVSNorton/Lincoln59.html.

Luther, Martin. "A Mighty Fortress Is Our God." 1852.

Mackman, Frank M. "Everett Dirksen's Last Days." The Dirksen Congressional Center. Pekin, Illinois. 2019.

Malone, Ryan C. *The Harmony of the Spheres.* Philadelphia. Church of God, August 11, 2016.

Miller, William Lee. *Lincoln's Virtues: An Ethical Biography.* New York: Vantage Books, 2002.

Sandburg, Carl, Edward C. Goodman ed. *Abraham Lincoln: The Prairie Years and The War Years.* New York: Sterling Publisher, 2007.

Signs of demonic activity based on a warning from a Catholic exorcist (the Lord be with you). Facebook photo. January 28, 2021. https://m.facebook.com.photos.

Smith, Robert Barr. "Were the Angels at Mons in WWI Real or Mass Hysteria?" Accessed 2023. https://warfarehistorynetwork.com.

The Occult: What Does the Bible Say? Christian Answers, 2023. https:// Christian Answers: net > of eden, edn-occult.

"What Is an Occult Bond?" Charis International, Doctrinal Commission. Accessed July 28, 2021.

Willis, Chuck. *The Presidential Archives.* New York: DK Publishing, 2007.

HOLY BIBLE, New Life Version, Christian Literature International, Canby OR, Copyright C 1969-2003

Holy Bible, King James Version, Public Domain, Bible Gateway, htttps://www.biblegateway

ABOUT THE AUTHOR

Born a Midwesterner in Evanston, Illinois, Dr. Chapman graduated from the University of Illinois with honors; earned a master's of criminal justice from the University of South Carolina, graduating as a distinguished honor graduate; and earned a Doctor of Ministry from the Chicago Theological Seminary. Educated as a scientific rationalist with some research experience, and retired after thirty-five years of ministry, Phil traveled the world as a chaplain in the US Army then served in the Federal Bureau of Prisons.

After some reticence, Dr. Chapman now chooses to share mystical experiences from his personal life and career. Dr. Chapman chronicles his experience with angels, déjà vu, ghosts, miracles, synchronistic phenomena, and visions. He provides a witness to God's providential care.

www.ingramcontent.com/pod-product-compliance
Lightning Source LLC
Chambersburg PA
CBHW071026120626
46546CB00003B/1237